The Twin Manifestations

Ruhi Institute

Books in the Series:

Below are the current titles in the series designed by the Ruhi Institute. The books are intended to be used as the main sequence of courses in a systematic effort to enhance the capacity of youth and adults to serve their communities. The Ruhi Institute is also developing a set of courses that branch out from the third book in the series for training Bahá'í children's classes teachers, and this is indicated in the list as well. It should be noted that the list will undergo change as experience in the field advances, and new titles will be added as an increasing number of curricular elements under development reach the stage where they can be made widely available.

Ruhi Institute
Apartado Postal: 402032
Cali, Colombia
Tel: 57 2 828-2599
Email: instituto@ruhi.org
Web site: www.ruhi.org

Contents

TO THE COLLABORATORS

Twenty-three May 1844 marked the beginning of a new era in human history. For centuries, all the peoples of the world have awaited the Promised Day of God, a Day when peace and harmony would be established on earth. The dawn of this new Day witnessed the appearance of not one but two Manifestations of God, the Báb and Bahá'u'lláh, Whose Revelations released the spiritual forces destined to transform society in accordance with the Will of God.

The life of a Manifestation of God is fundamentally different from that of other human beings, and His greatness cannot be comprehended through a mere study of the events surrounding Him. During the years that He lives on earth, His extraordinary powers are diffused over the entire planet, causing a profound change in the reality of all created things and preparing humanity for a new stage of progress. Though to external eyes His life may appear to be filled with afflictions, spiritual eyes discern in each event the signs of His glory and majesty.

In the curriculum of the Ruhi Institute, the three units that comprise Book 4 are devoted to helping students acquire a thorough and systematic knowledge of the lives of the Báb and Bahá'u'lláh. A chronological account of each of Their lives is presented—in units 2 and 3 respectively—and it is hoped that the students will learn to narrate them in some detail. These chronological narratives, particularly in the unit on the life of Bahá'u'lláh, are complemented by passages from the Writings that illuminate certain of the spiritual themes associated with the person of the Manifestation. Several of these passages are followed by exercises, while others merely ask for repeated reading and personal reflection.

The first unit of the book is meant to prepare the participants of the course for the study of the historical accounts. It consists of several passages from the Writings that speak of the greatness of this Day, and a few simple exercises.

In working with groups of students, tutors are asked to place equal emphasis on both aspects of the material presented in the book: the insights offered into spiritual matters as well as the knowledge conveyed about the history of the Faith. One important concept treated in the third unit is that of crisis and victory. The understanding of this concept is essential for every Bahá'í in order to appreciate the history of the Faith and also to contribute to its expansion and consolidation, processes which invariably go through a series of crises and victories.

Furthermore, the ability to narrate the story of the Báb and Bahá'u'lláh in a way that touches the listener's heart should be given importance. The necessary skills can only be developed through repeated study of the material and with the assistance of a loving tutor. To help the participants give a first very simple presentation, a booklet consisting of drawings and brief captions is included in each of the two units of history. If need be, these may be copied and used separately along with other visual aids in campaigns of large-scale expansion and consolidation.

The Greatness of This Day

Purpose

To gain spiritual insights into
the significance of this Day
and the promises it holds
for humanity.

SECTION 1

As Bahá'ís, we are blessed with the knowledge that we live in a very special Day, a Day in which two Manifestations of God have appeared and renewed all created things. We see, before our very own eyes, how the forces released by these Manifestations are changing human society—how an old world is passing away and a new one being established in its place. It is, of course, true that the dying of a world brings with it untold suffering. We are deeply affected by this suffering and saddened by the destruction around us, but we are not overwhelmed, for we recognize that the world is moving rapidly towards that which Bahá'u'lláh has destined for it.

To live in such a Day, the Day of God, is a bounty beyond measure, but it brings with it weighty responsibilities. To appreciate this bounty and discharge our duties, we must ponder often on the significance and greatness of this Day. 'Abdu'l-Bahá has said that man can withstand anything except that which God has willed for this age. Is it not essential for every Bahá'í, then, to become increasingly aware of God's purpose for humanity today, a purpose the fulfillment of which the powers of earth cannot prevent? The aim of this unit, which is relatively short, is to familiarize you with some of the passages from the Writings that refer to the greatness of the Day in which we live. Before studying these passages and reflecting on their meaning, you will find it helpful to consult with your group on the following:

1.   The unification of the human race is one of the goals that, according to God's Will, is to be achieved in this age. What are some of the other accomplishments that God has purposed for humanity today? _____

_____

_____

_____

_____

_____

2.   'Abdu'l-Bahá has said that man cannot withstand that which God has intended for humanity today. Give some examples of those "powers of earth" that try to prevent the fulfillment of God's purpose. _____

_____

_____

_____

_____

_____

3.   In what ways do these "powers of earth" try to prevent humanity from accomplishing that which God has destined for it? _____

_____

_____

_____

_____

_____

4.   Can you give examples from the history of the Faith in order to illustrate that
     the efforts of these "powers" will always end in failure? _____

     _____

     _____

     _____

     _____

     _____

SECTION 2

Bahá'u'lláh says:

> **"Verily I say, this is the Day in which mankind can behold the Face, and hear
> the Voice, of the Promised One. The Call of God hath been raised, and the
> light of His countenance hath been lifted up upon men. It behooveth every
> man to blot out the trace of every idle word from the tablet of his heart, and
> to gaze, with an open and unbiased mind, on the signs of His Revelation, the
> proofs of His Mission, and the tokens of His glory."** [1]

Exercises:

1.   Complete the following sentences:

     a.   In this Day, we can see the _____, and hear the _____,
          of the Promised One.

     b.   _____ has been raised, and the _____
          of His _____ has been lifted up upon us.

     c.   It is our duty to erase from our _____ the _____
          of every _____, and to gaze, with an _____
          and _____ mind, on the _____ of His
          Revelation, the _____ of His Mission, and the _____
          of His glory.

2.	Which of the following are idle words that prevent people from recognizing Bahá'u'lláh?

_____ The religion of my parents is good enough for me.

_____ Humanity is in need of a spiritual springtime.

_____ Religion is fine for those who need it.

_____ Religion is only a cause of conflict, so it should be done away with.

_____ As far as I can see, all religions are more or less the same, so it doesn't make any difference to which you belong.

_____ God has abandoned humanity.

_____ All things have to be made new, including religion.

_____ Science proves that there is no God. All our problems can be solved if we use the power of reason.

_____ I don't want to commit myself to any religion.

_____ Every individual should be allowed to know God in his or her own way. Why do we need a Manifestation?

_____ We have the Holy Scriptures of our own religion. There is no need for a new Manifestation.

3.	Which of the following are among the signs of Bahá'u'lláh's Revelation, the proofs of His Mission, and the tokens of His glory?

_____ The power of His Covenant.

_____ The penetrating power of His Words.

_____ The transformation of the hearts of those who come into contact with His Writings.

_____ The influence His Teachings have on people's thoughts and actions.

_____ The influence His Teachings have on the direction of history.

_____ The eloquence of His utterance.

_____ The validity of the statements He made about the future.

_____ His long-suffering, His tribulations and His woe.

_____ His sovereignty in spite of being a victim of oppression by earthly powers.

_____ His ability to unite people of every race and creed.

_____ The steady growth of the community of His followers.

_____ The courage and exquisite qualities of those who joyfully gave their lives for His Cause.

_____ The magnificence of His Administrative Order.

_____ The way the world is moving towards that which He designed.

_____ The way the principles of His Faith are becoming universally accepted.

4. When one thinks about a soul recognizing Bahá'u'lláh, many images come to mind. Fill in the blanks with the appropriate words: wakefulness, certitude, light, awareness, trust, strength.

    a. The passage from darkness to _____

    b. The passage from slumber to _____

    c. The passage from heedlessness to _____

    d. The passage from helplessness to _____

    e. The passage from suspicion to _____

    f. The passage from doubt to _____

SECTION 3

Bahá'u'lláh says:

> **"This is the Day in which God's most excellent favors have been poured out upon men, the Day in which His most mighty grace hath been infused into all created things. It is incumbent upon all the peoples of the world to reconcile their differences, and, with perfect unity and peace, abide beneath the shadow of the Tree of His care and loving-kindness. It behooveth them to cleave to whatsoever will, in this Day, be conducive to the exaltation of their stations, and to the promotion of their best interests."** [2]

Exercises:

1. Complete the following sentences:

    a. In this Day, God's most excellent _____ have been _____ _____ upon men.

    b. In this Day, God's most mighty _____ has been _____ into all created things.

c. All the peoples of the world must _____ their _____, and, with _____ and _____, abide beneath the shadow of the _____ of His _____ and _____.

d. The peoples of the world should hold fast to whatsoever will be conducive to the _____ of their _____, and to the _____ of their _____.

2. What are some of the "most excellent favors" that God has bestowed upon humanity in this Day? _____

_____

_____

_____

_____

_____

3. What does the word "conducive" mean? _____

4. Make a list of those things you can do to promote humanity's best interests.

_____

_____

_____

_____

_____

_____

_____

_____

_____

_____

_____

_____

_____

_____

_____

_____

_____

_____

_____

_____

SECTION 4

Bahá'u'lláh says:

> **"This is the Day whereon the Ocean of God's mercy hath been manifested unto men, the Day in which the Day Star of His loving-kindness hath shed its radiance upon them, the Day in which the clouds of His bountiful favor have overshadowed the whole of mankind. Now is the time to cheer and refresh the down-cast through the invigorating breeze of love and fellowship, and the living waters of friendliness and charity."** [3]

Exercises:

1.   Complete the following sentences:

   a.   In this Day, the Ocean of God's _____ has been _____ _____.

   b.   In this Day, the Day Star of His _____ has _____ its _____.

   c.   In this Day, the clouds of His _____ have _____ the whole of mankind.

   d.   _____ is the time to _____ and _____ the down-cast through the invigorating breeze of _____ and _____, and the living waters of _____ and _____.

2.   Which of the following cheer and refresh the down-cast?

   _____ Helping them gain access to education.

   _____ Helping them to increase their capacity to consult.

   _____ Collecting food and clothing for them.

   _____ Bringing the results of science to bear on their lives.

   _____ Getting them involved in political parties.

   _____ Sharing with them the Word of God.

   _____ Talking them into buying something they don't need on credit.

_____ Increasing their awareness of the importance of prayer.

_____ Encouraging them in their worthy endeavors.

_____ Helping them to present their grievances eloquently to the authorities through legal means.

_____ Organizing protest meetings for them.

_____ Selling alcohol to them so that they can forget their problems.

_____ Bringing to them the benefits of a health-care system.

_____ Setting up a discotheque in their midst so that they can have fun.

_____ Teaching them so that they can recognize the Manifestation of God for today.

_____ Helping them to appreciate the power of divine assistance.

SECTION 5

Bahá'u'lláh says:

> **"Great indeed is this Day! The allusions made to it in all the sacred Scriptures as the Day of God attest its greatness. The soul of every Prophet of God, of every Divine Messenger, hath thirsted for this wondrous Day. All the divers kindreds of the earth have, likewise, yearned to attain it. No sooner, however, had the Day Star of His Revelation manifested itself in the heaven of God's Will, than all, except those whom the Almighty was pleased to guide, were found dumbfounded and heedless."** [4]

Exercises:

1.   Complete the following sentences:

   a.   _____ indeed is this Day! The allusions made to it in all the
        _____ as the _____
        attest its _____.

   b.   The soul of every _____ of God, of every _____
        _____, has _____ for this _____
        Day.

c. All the _____ of the earth have, likewise,

_____ to _____ it.

d. No sooner had the Day Star of His Revelation _____
itself, than all, except those whom the _____ was
_____ to _____, were found _____
and _____.

2. From the quotation above, it is clear that this is the day of fulfillment. All the Prophets and Messengers of God have foretold the coming of the Day when the Most Great Peace would be established on earth. Yet when the Promise of All Ages appeared, only a few responded to His call. Most remained in a state of slumber, while others arose with fanaticism and hatred to persecute Him. It is important, then, to pause and consider why such souls were kept back from recognizing the Promised One, even though they were eagerly awaiting His coming. Discuss this question in your group and try to identify some of the reasons. Write your conclusions in the space below.

_____

_____

_____

_____

_____

_____

_____

_____

_____

_____

_____

_____

_____

_____

_____

3. Now, in your own heart, consider the following questions: Why do you think you were able to recognize Bahá'u'lláh? What can you do to show your gratitude for having received such a bounty?

SECTION 6

Bahá'u'lláh says:

> **"The world's equilibrium hath been upset through the vibrating influence of this most great, this new World Order. Mankind's ordered life hath been revolutionized through the agency of this unique, this wondrous System—the like of which mortal eyes have never witnessed.**

> **"Immerse yourselves in the ocean of My words, that ye may unravel its secrets, and discover all the pearls of wisdom that lie hid in its depths. Take heed that ye do not vacillate in your determination to embrace the truth of this Cause—a Cause through which the potentialities of the might of God have been revealed, and His sovereignty established." [5]**

Exercises:

1.   Complete the following sentences:

   a.   The world's _____ has been _____ through
        the vibrating _____ of this most great, this _____
        _____.

   b.   Mankind's _____ has been _____
        through the agency of this _____, this wondrous _____.

   c.   We should _____ ourselves in the _____ of His
        words, that we may _____ its _____ , and
        _____ all the pearls of _____ that lie hid
        in its depths.

   d.   We should not _____ in our _____ to
        embrace the _____ of this Cause.

   e.   This is a Cause through which the _____ of the
        _____ of God have been _____ , and His
        _____ established.

2.   What does the word "equilibrium" mean? _____

3.   What has upset the world's equilibrium? _____
     _____

4. What are some of the signs indicating that the world has lost its equilibrium? _____

_____

_____

_____

_____

_____

_____

5. What are some of the signs indicating that humanity's life has been revolutionized?

_____

_____

_____

_____

_____

6. What is the "wondrous System" to which Bahá'u'lláh refers? _____

_____

7. How do we immerse ourselves in the ocean of Bahá'u'lláh's words? _____

_____

_____

8. How are our thoughts affected when we immerse ourselves in the ocean of His words?

_____

_____

_____

9. How are our actions affected when we immerse ourselves in the ocean of His words?

_____

_____

_____

10. From where do we receive the spiritual energy required to work for the establishment of the World Order of Bahá'u'lláh? _____

_____

11. What does the word "vacillate" mean? _____

12.   How is our spiritual energy affected if we vacillate in accepting the Truth of His Cause in its entirety? _____

_____

_____

_____

_____

SECTION 7

'Abdu'l-Bahá says:

"O ye beloved of the Lord! This day is the day of union, the day of the ingathering of all mankind. 'Verily God loveth those who, as though they were a solid wall, do battle for His Cause in serried lines!' Note that He saith 'in serried lines'—meaning crowded and pressed together, one locked to the next, each supporting his fellows. To do battle, as stated in the sacred verse, doth not, in this greatest of all dispensations, mean to go forth with sword and spear, with lance and piercing arrow—but rather weaponed with pure intent, with righteous motives, with counsels helpful and effective, with godly attributes, with deeds pleasing to the Almighty, with the qualities of heaven. It signifieth education for all mankind, guidance for all men, the spreading far and wide of the sweet savors of the spirit, the promulgation of God's proofs, the setting forth of arguments conclusive and divine, the doing of charitable deeds." [6]

Exercises:

1.   Complete the following sentences:

a.   'Abdu'l-Bahá tells us that this day is the day of _____, the day of the _____ of all _____.

b.   He explains that God _____ those who, as though they were a _____ do _____ for His Cause in _____.

c.   To be "in serried lines", 'Abdu'l-Bahá explains, means to be _____ and _____, one _____ to the next, each _____ his fellows.

d.   To do battle in service to the Cause in this greatest of all _____,

He tells us, does not mean to go forth with _____ and _____, with _____ and _____—but rather _____ with _____, with _____ _____, with _____, with _____, with _____ _____, with _____.

e. Likewise, to do battle in this dispensation signifies _____ for all mankind, _____ for all men, the _____ far and wide of the _____ of the _____, the _____ of God's _____, the _____ _____ of _____, the _____ of _____.

2. This is the day of the unification of the human race. To appreciate how great is this task, think of the countless different divisions by which human beings have separated themselves. Make a list of as many as you can.

_____

_____

_____

_____

_____

_____

_____

_____

_____

_____

_____

_____

_____

_____

_____

_____

3. What power can unite all these contending peoples?_____

_____

4. What is the nature of the battle in which we are engaged?_____

_____

5.   How are we to fight in this battle? _____

6.   Put a check next to the weapons that are to be used in this battle:

_____ Pure intent	_____ Anger
_____ Godly attributes	_____ Generosity
_____ Germ warfare	_____ The power of prayer
_____ Righteous motives	_____ Praiseworthy deeds
_____ A desire to be a leader of men	_____ The love of God
_____ Arrogance and pride	_____ Love for humanity
_____ Passion for justice	_____ Trust in God
_____ Self-righteousness	_____ A desire to make a profit
_____ Chemical warfare	_____ Encouragement
_____ Guns	_____ Helpful and effective advice
_____ Knives	_____ Nuclear weapons
_____ The power of the Word of God	_____ Money
_____ Self-satisfaction	_____ Faith
_____ A desire to manipulate others in order to improve their character	_____ A desire to dominate others in order to establish justice

7.   Which of the following represent the things we do when we are engaged in this battle?

_____ Perform charitable deeds.

_____ Educate others.

_____ Force others to do what we want.

_____ Teach the Cause of God.

_____ Proclaim the Cause of God.

_____ Divide into factions according to our own interests.

_____ Fight for the interests of the group to which we belong.

_____ Set forth conclusive arguments of the Truth of Bahá'u'lláh's Revelation.

_____ Immerse ourselves in the ocean of His Words.

_____ Oppress the weak and the down-trodden.

_____ Pray ardently.

_____ Plunder people's possessions.

_____ Accumulate wealth by stealing from others.

SECTION 8

Undoubtedly your awareness of the greatness of this Day has increased through the study of the preceding passages. Such a heightened awareness creates in all of us a desire to arise, to teach, to serve, and to perform sacrificial deeds. So as not to lose sight of the urgency with which you must engage in acts of service to the Cause, commit to memory the following passage from a letter dated 28 January 1939 written by the Guardian:

"There is no time to lose. There is no room left for vacillation. Multitudes hunger for the Bread of Life. The stage is set. The firm and irrevocable Promise is given. God's own Plan has been set in motion. It is gathering momentum with every passing day. The powers of heaven and earth mysteriously assist in its execution. Such an opportunity is irreplaceable. Let the doubter arise, and himself verify the truth of such assertions. To try, to persevere, is to insure ultimate and complete victory."[7]

REFERENCES

1.   *Gleanings from the Writings of Bahá'u'lláh* (Wilmette: Bahá'í Publishing Trust, 1994), VII, pp. 10-11.

2.   Ibid., IV, p. 6.

3.   Ibid., V, p. 7.

4.   Ibid., VII, p. 11.

5.   Ibid., LXX, p. 136.

6.   *Selections from the Writings of 'Abdu'l-Bahá* (Haifa: Bahá'í World Centre, 1982), no. 207, p. 260.

7.   *Messages to America: Selected Letters and Cablegrams Addressed to the Bahá'ís of North America, 1932-1946* (Wilmette: Bahá'í Publishing Committee, 1947), p. 17.

The Life of the Báb

Purpose

To learn to narrate the story of the Báb's life
and gain an appreciation of the potency of
His short and dramatic Ministry.

Practice

Visit a few families and share with them
a simple illustrated presentation of the Báb's life.

SECTION 1

The Dispensation of the Báb began in 1844 and lasted only nine years. Its primary purpose was to prepare the way for the coming of Bahá'u'lláh. Although brief, the Báb's Dispensation was of such tremendous spiritual intensity that its effect will be felt for hundreds of generations to come.

The Báb, Whose name was Siyyid 'Alí-Muḥammad, was born on 20 October 1819 in Shíráz, a city in southern Iran, also known as Persia. Most of the people in Iran belong to a sect of Islám that awaits the coming of a Promised One of God called the Qá'im. The word "Qá'im" means He who ariseth.

The Báb belonged to a distinguished and noble family that traced its ancestry to Muḥammad, the Prophet of Islám. His father passed away when He was a small child, and He was raised by His maternal uncle, who placed Him in school at an early age. Although the Báb was endowed with innate knowledge and did not need to be instructed by any man, He followed His uncle's wishes. His teacher, however, quickly recognized the Báb's great capacity and realized he had nothing to teach this extraordinary child. He has told the following story about the Báb's school days:

> "One day I asked the Báb to recite the opening words of the Qur'án . . . He hesitated, pleading that unless He were told what the words signified, He would in no wise attempt to pronounce them. I pretended not to know their meaning. 'I know what these words signify,' observed my pupil; 'by your leave, I will explain them.' He spoke with such knowledge and fluency that I was struck with amazement. . . . The sweetness of His utterance still lingers in my memory. I felt impelled to take Him back to His uncle and to deliver into his hands the Trust he had committed to my care. I determined to tell him how unworthy I felt to teach so remarkable a child. I found His uncle alone in his office. 'I have brought Him back to you,' I said, 'and commit Him to your vigilant protection. He is not to be treated as a mere child, for in Him I can already discern evidences of that mysterious power which the Revelation of the Qá'im alone can reveal. It is incumbent upon you to surround Him with your most loving care. Keep Him in your house, for He, verily, stands in no need of teachers such as I.' His uncle sternly rebuked the Báb. 'Have you forgotten my instructions?' he said. 'Have I not already admonished You to follow the example of Your fellow-pupils, to observe silence, and to listen attentively to every word spoken by Your teacher?' Having obtained His promise to abide faithfully by his instructions, he bade the Báb return to His school. The soul of that child could not, however, be restrained by the stern admonitions of His uncle. No discipline could repress the flow of His intuitive knowledge. Day after day He continued to manifest such remarkable evidences of superhuman wisdom as I am powerless to recount." [1]

At last the Báb's uncle decided to allow Him to leave school. He then began to work with His uncle as a merchant in Búshihr, a city southwest of Shíráz. It was in this period of His life that the Báb married. He and His wife had a son named Aḥmad, who died in infancy the year before the Báb declared Himself to be the Promised Qá'im.

During His youth, the Báb showed signs of a power and greatness that no one could rival. The extraordinary qualities that would distinguish Him throughout His swift and tragic Ministry were already manifest. The Guardian refers to Him as **"the gentle, the youthful and irresistible person of the Báb, matchless in His meekness, imperturbable in His serenity, magnetic in His utterance"**. [2] The sections that follow can but inadequately describe the events of His life. Yet even this brief account should ignite in our hearts a spark from the fire of love that He enkindled in the hearts of thousands and thousands of His followers.

Exercises:

1. What was the Báb's name? _____

2. Where was the Báb born and on what date? _____

_____

3. What does the word "Qá'im" mean? _HE WHO ARISETH_

4. To whom did the family of the Báb trace its ancestry? _MUHAMAD_

5. Who was responsible for raising the Báb after His father passed away? _____
   _MATERNAL UNCLE_____

6. What is meant by the statement that the Báb was endowed by God with innate knowledge? _____

_____

7. What did the teacher of the Báb think when he recognized His great capacity?_____

_____

8. What is the Qur'án? _____

9. What does the phrase "superhuman wisdom" mean? _____

_____

10. What did the Báb do after leaving school? _____

_____

11. Write in your own words the story of the Báb's school days, as told by His teacher.

_____

_____

_____

_____

_____

_____

_____

_____

_____

_____

_____

_____

_____

_____

_____

_____

SECTION 2

Before the Báb declared His Mission, several people around the world knew deep in their hearts that the Promised One would soon appear. One of these saintly personages was Siyyid Káẓim, who lived in the city of Karbilá in 'Iráq. Siyyid Káẓim had many students, and he devoted his life to preparing them for the long-awaited coming of the Qá'im. He repeatedly told them that after his death they should leave their homes and, with hearts free of all earthly desires, spread out in search of the Promised Beloved.

After the passing of Siyyid Káẓim, a most distinguished student of his, Mullá Ḥusayn, went to a mosque and spent forty days in prayer and meditation, during which he opened wide his heart to God's inspiration. Having completed these forty days, he left 'Iráq with two companions and set out in search of the Promised One. He went first to Búshihr. But he did not remain there long, for something seemed to pull him irresistibly northwards, and he soon departed for Shíráz. Arriving at the gate of that city, he instructed his two companions to go directly to the mosque and remain there until his arrival.

A few hours before sunset on that very day, while walking outside the gate of the city, he met a youthful Personage Who welcomed him and invited him to His home to refresh himself after his long and difficult journey. Mullá Ḥusayn was deeply impressed by the gentle yet compelling manner in which this extraordinary Youth spoke. He followed Him, and soon they arrived at the gate of a modest house. They entered the house and were seated in the upper room. The gracious Host ordered a water-jug to be brought so that His guest could wash away the dust from his journey. Then, He Himself prepared tea and offered it to Mullá Ḥusayn. After these acts of hospitality, He began to speak with His guest. The details of that historic conversation were later told by Mullá Ḥusayn:

"It was about an hour after sunset when my youthful Host began to converse with me. 'Whom, after Siyyid Káẓim,' He asked me, 'do you regard as his successor and your leader?' 'At the hour of his death,' I replied, 'our departed teacher insistently exhorted us to forsake our homes, to scatter far and wide, in quest of the Promised Beloved. I have, accordingly, journeyed to Persia, have arisen to accomplish his will, and am still engaged in my quest.' 'Has your teacher,' He further inquired, 'given you any detailed indications as to the distinguishing features of the Promised One?' 'Yes,' I replied, 'He is of a pure lineage, is of illustrious descent, and of the seed of Fáṭimih. As to His age, He is more than twenty and less than thirty. He is endowed with innate knowledge. He is of medium height, abstains from smoking, and is free from bodily deficiency.' He paused for a while and then with vibrant voice declared: 'Behold, all these signs are manifest in Me!' He then considered each of the above-mentioned signs separately, and conclusively demonstrated that each and all were applicable to His person." [3]

During that night, the Báb demonstrated to Mullá Ḥusayn, with clear and unmistakable proofs, that He was the Promised Qá'im. He revealed, with extraordinary rapidity, the first part of His commentary on the Súrih of Joseph, an important chapter of the Qur'án. He then addressed Mullá Ḥusayn in these words:

"O thou who art the first to believe in Me! Verily I say, I am the Báb, the Gate of God, and thou art the Bábu'l-Báb, the gate of that Gate. Eighteen souls must, in the beginning, spontaneously and of their own accord, accept Me and recognize the truth of My Revelation. Unwarned and uninvited, each of these must seek independently to find Me. And when their number is complete, one of them must needs be chosen to accompany Me on My pilgrimage to Mecca and Medina. There I shall deliver the Message of God to the Sharíf of Mecca. I then shall return to Kúfih, where again, in the mosque of that holy city, I shall manifest His Cause. It is incumbent upon you not to divulge, either to your companions or to any other soul, that which you have seen and heard." [4]

This glorious Revelation filled Mullá Ḥusayn's soul with excitement and joy, with awe and wonder. "How feeble and impotent, how dejected and timid, I had felt previously!" he later said. "Then I could neither write nor walk, so tremulous were my hands and feet. Now, however, the knowledge of His Revelation had galvanized my being. I felt possessed of such courage and power that were the world, all its peoples and its potentates, to rise against me, I would, alone and undaunted, withstand their onslaught. The universe seemed but a handful of dust in my grasp. I seemed to be the Voice of Gabriel personified, calling unto all mankind: 'Awake, for, lo! the morning Light has broken. Arise, for His Cause is made manifest. The portal of His grace is open wide; enter therein, O peoples of the world! For He Who is your Promised One is come!'" [5]

The Declaration of the Báb took place on the eve of 23 May 1844. He was twenty-five years old. Many years later on the occasion of the anniversary of the Báb's Declaration, 'Abdu'l-Bahá addressed a group of believers in the following words:

"This is 23 May, the anniversary of the message and Declaration of the Báb. It is a blessed day and the dawn of manifestation, for the appearance of the Báb was the early light of the true morn, . . . it is a blessed day, the inception of the heavenly bounty, the beginning of the divine effulgence. On this day in 1844 the Báb was sent forth heralding and proclaiming the Kingdom of God, announcing the glad tidings of the coming of Bahá'u'lláh and withstanding the opposition of the whole Persian nation." [6]

Exercises:

1. Mention the name of the holy person who was preparing the way for the Báb's coming just before His Declaration. _____ .

2. Siyyid Kázim repeatedly told his students that after his death they should _____ their _____ and, with hearts _____ of all _____ desires, _____ in search of the _____ .

3. One of Siyyid Kázim's most distinguished students was _____ _____

4. What did Mullá Ḥusayn do after the passing of Siyyid Kázim? _____ _____

5. Write four sentences, each of which includes at least two of the following words: Islám, Muslim, Qur'án, mosque, Medina, Mecca.

   a. _____
   b. _____
   c. _____
   d. _____

6. How did the Báb know that Mullá Ḥusayn had arrived in S̲h̲íráz? _____ _____

7. What questions did the Báb ask Mullá Ḥusayn after they arrived at His home?

   a. _____
      _____
   b. _____
      _____

8. What description had Siyyid Kázim given his students so that they would be able to recognize the Qá'im?

   "He is of a ___PURE LINEAGE___, is of _____, and of the _____ . As to His age, He is _____ than _____ and _____ than _____ . He is endowed with _____ . He is of _____ _____, abstains from _____, and is free from _____ _____ ."

9. Who is Fátimih? _____

10. Did the Báb possess the qualities that Mullá Ḥusayn was searching for? _____

11. What does the title "the Báb" mean? _____

12. What title did the Báb give to Mullá Ḥusayn? _____

13. What does this title mean? _____

14. What did the Báb tell Mullá Ḥusayn would have to happen before He would openly proclaim His Cause? _____

    _____

    _____

15. Mullá Ḥusayn described in the following words how he felt after having received the Báb's Revelation: "How _____ and _____, how _____ and _____, I had felt previously! Then I could neither _____ nor _____, so _____ were my hands and feet. Now, however, the _____ of His _____ had _____ my being. I felt possessed of such _____ and _____ that were the _____, all its _____ and its _____, to rise _____ me, I would, _____ and _____, _____ their onslaught.

16. When did the Báb's Declaration take place? _____

17. How old was the Báb at the time of His Declaration? _____

SECTION 3

After Mullá Ḥusayn, seventeen other individuals sought and independently found their Heart's Desire, the Báb. Each was guided by God to recognize the truth of the newborn Revelation, some through visions or dreams, some through prayer, and others during moments of meditation. All but one of these blessed souls attained the Báb's presence in Shíráz. The one who did not meet Him was a unique and talented woman called Ṭáhirih. She came to know of the Báb through a dream, recognized Him as the Promised Beloved and became a great promoter of His Cause. The eighteenth person to join the ranks of His followers was a twenty-two year old youth known as Quddús. Although young, Quddús possessed an exemplary character, and courage and faith that few could equal. These first believers, together with Mullá Ḥusayn, were declared by the Báb as the eighteen "Letters of the Living". They were His chosen apostles.

Soon after the number of the Letters of the Living was complete, the Báb called Mullá Ḥusayn to His presence and gave him the following instructions:

"The days of our companionship are approaching their end. My Covenant with you is now accomplished. Gird up the loins of endeavor, and arise to diffuse My Cause. Be not dismayed at the sight of the degeneracy and perversity of this generation, for the Lord of the Covenant shall assuredly assist you. Verily, He shall surround you with His loving protection, and shall lead you from victory to victory. Even as the cloud that rains its bounty upon the earth, traverse the land from end to end, and shower upon its people the blessings which the Almighty, in His mercy, has deigned to confer upon you. . . . In this pilgrimage upon which We are soon to embark, We have chosen Quddús as Our companion. We have left you behind to face the onslaught of a fierce and relentless enemy. Rest assured, however, that a bounty unspeakably glorious shall be conferred upon you. Follow the course of your journey towards the north, and visit on your way Iṣfáhán, Káshán, Qum, and Ṭihrán. Beseech almighty Providence that He may graciously enable you to attain, in that capital, the seat of true sovereignty, and to enter the mansion of the Beloved. A secret lies hidden in that city. When made manifest, it shall turn the earth into paradise. My hope is that you may partake of its grace and recognize its splendor." [7]

Having given Mullá Ḥusayn instructions to go to Ṭihrán, the Báb summoned the other Letters of the Living to His presence and assigned to each one a special mission. In His parting words to them, He called upon them to lay aside every earthly desire and scatter far and wide to proclaim His Cause. "O My beloved friends!" He addressed them. "You are the bearers of the name of God in this Day . . . It behooves each one of you to manifest the attributes of God, and to exemplify by your deeds and words the signs of His righteousness, His power and glory." "Heed not your weaknesses and frailty," He assured them. "Fix your gaze upon the invincible power of the Lord, your God, the Almighty. . . . Arise in His name, put your trust wholly in Him, and be assured of ultimate victory." [8]

In October 1844 the Báb, accompanied by Quddús, set out on His pilgrimage to Mecca and Medina. These two cities, located in Arabia, are sacred for the followers of Islám. While in Mecca, the Báb wrote a letter to the Sharíf of the city. In that letter, He clearly explained His Mission and called upon the Sharíf to accept His Cause. But the Sharíf, who was busy with his own affairs, failed to respond to the Divine Messenger. From Mecca, the Báb went with His companion to Medina, where the mortal remains of the Prophet Muḥammad are enshrined. After visiting that holy city, they made their way back to Persia. Arriving in Búshihr, the Báb summoned Quddús to His presence and with these words instructed him to proceed to Shíráz:

"The days of your companionship with Me are drawing to a close. The hour of separation has struck, a separation which no reunion will follow except in the Kingdom of God . . . In the streets of Shíráz, indignities will be heaped upon you, and the severest injuries will afflict your body. You will survive the ignominious behavior of your foes, and will attain the presence of Him who is the one object of our adoration and love. In His presence you will forget all the harm and disgrace that shall have befallen you. The hosts of the Unseen will hasten forth to assist you, and will proclaim to all the world your heroism and glory. Yours will be the ineffable joy of quaffing the cup of martyrdom for His sake. I, too, shall tread the path of sacrifice, and will join you in the realm of eternity." [9]

Exercises:

1. What title did the Báb give to the first believers who recognized Him as the Promised One? _____

2. How many were there? _____

3. Who was the first one to recognize the Báb? _____

4. Who was the last Letter of the Living? _____

5. How were the Letters of the Living guided to recognize the truth of the Báb's Revelation? _____

    _____

6. Which of the Letters of the Living did not attain the Báb's presence? _____

7. Whom did the Báb choose to accompany Him on pilgrimage? _____

8. Soon after the number of the Letters of the Living was complete, the Báb called Mullá Ḥusayn to His presence and gave him the following instructions: "The days of our _____ are _____ their _____.
   My _____ with you is now _____. _____
   the loins of _____, and _____ to diffuse My _____.
   Be not _____ at the _____ of the _____
   and _____ of this _____, for the _____ of the
   _____ shall _____ _____ you. Verily, He
   shall _____ you with His loving _____, and
   shall lead you from _____ to _____. Even as the
   _____ that rains its bounty upon the earth, _____ the land from
   end to end, and _____ upon its people the _____
   which the _____, in His mercy, has deigned to confer upon you."

9. What route did the Báb tell Mullá Ḥusayn to take on his journey? _____

    _____

10. Memorize the following:

    "Beseech almighty Providence that He may graciously enable you to attain, in that capital, the seat of true sovereignty, and to enter the mansion of the Beloved. A secret lies hidden in that city. When made manifest, it shall turn the earth into paradise. My hope is that you may partake of its grace and recognize its splendor." [7]

11. What secret was hidden in Ṭihrán? _____

12. After directing Mullá Ḥusayn to go to Ṭihrán, what instructions did the Báb give to the other Letters of the Living? _____

_____

13. When did the Báb set out on His pilgrimage? _____

14. To what cities did the Báb go on His pilgrimage? _____

15. To whom did He write in Mecca? _____

16. Why is Medina a holy city for Muslims? _____

_____

17. What does the word "enshrined" mean? _____

_____

18. In the space below, write what the Báb told Quddús when they reached Búshihr.

_____

_____

_____

_____

_____

_____

_____

_____

_____

_____

19. Whom did the Báb promise Quddús he would meet? _____

_____

SECTION 4

In Shíráz, Quddús began teaching the new Message with great fervor. But soon he faced opposition from the Islamic clergy and the governor of the province. The governor, a cruel and wicked man, ordered the arrest of Quddús and one of his companions. He commanded that their beards should be burned, that their noses be pierced with a hole through which a cord be passed, and that with this cord they should be led through the streets for all to see. "It will be an object lesson to the people of Shíráz," was the decree of the governor, "who will know what the penalty of heresy will be." [10] After suffering these indignities, Quddús and his companion were expelled from the city, being warned they would be put to death if they attempted to return. By their suffering, these two heroic souls earned the honor of having been the first to be persecuted in Persia for the sake of their new Faith. 'Abdu'l-Bahá has referred to the thousands who were later persecuted in the path of their Beloved, the Báb, in these words:

> **". . . they suffered the most grievous difficulties and severe ordeals. They with-stood the tests with wonderful power and sublime heroism. Thousands were cast into prison, punished, persecuted and martyred. Their homes were pillaged and destroyed, their possessions confiscated. They sacrificed their lives most willingly and remained unshaken in their faith to the very end. Those wonderful souls are the lamps of God, the stars of sanctity shining gloriously from the eternal horizon of the will of God." [11]**

Having ordered so unjust a punishment to be given to Quddús and his companion, the governor turned his anger towards the Báb. He sent his guards on horseback to Búshihr with instructions to arrest Him and to bring Him in chains to Shíráz. In the meantime, the Báb had left Búshihr for Shíráz. It was in the wilderness between these two cities that the mounted escort met Him. Much later, the leader of the escort told the story of that encounter:

"As we approached him, he saluted us and inquired as to our destination. I thought it best to conceal from him the truth, and replied that in this vicinity we had been commanded by the governor to conduct a certain inquiry. He smilingly observed: 'The governor has sent you to arrest Me. Here am I; do with Me as you please. By coming out to meet you, I have curtailed the length of your march, and have made it easier for you to find Me.' I was startled by his remarks and marvelled at his candor and straightforwardness. I could not explain, however, his readiness to subject himself, of his own accord, to the severe discipline of government officials, and to risk thereby his own life and safety. I tried to ignore him, and was preparing to leave, when he approached me and said: 'I swear by the righteousness of Him who created man, distinguished him from among the rest of His creatures, and caused his heart to be made the seat of His sovereignty and knowledge, that all My life I have uttered no word but the truth, and had no other desire except the welfare and advancement of My fellow-men. I have disdained My own ease and have avoided being the cause of pain or sorrow to anyone. I know that you are seeking Me. I prefer to deliver Myself into your hands, rather than subject you and your companions to unnecessary annoyance for My sake.' These words moved me profoundly. I instinctively dismounted from my horse, and, kissing his stirrups, addressed him in these words: 'O light of the eyes of the Prophet of God! I adjure you, by Him who has created you and endowed you with such loftiness and power, to grant my request and to answer my prayer. I beseech you to escape from this place and to flee from the ruthless and despicable governor of this province. I dread his machinations against you; I rebel at the idea of being made the instrument of his malignant designs against so innocent and noble a descendant of the Prophet of God. . . .' To my earnest entreaty he gave this answer: 'May the Lord your God requite you for your magnanimity and noble intention. No one knows the mystery of My Cause; no one can fathom its secrets. Never will I turn My face away from the decree of God. He alone is My sure Stronghold, My Stay and My Refuge. Until My last hour is at hand, none dare assail Me, none can frustrate the plan of the Almighty. And when My hour is come, how great will be My joy to quaff the cup of martyrdom in His name! Here am I; deliver Me into the hands of your master. Be not afraid, for no one will blame you.' I bowed my consent and carried out his desire." [12]

The Báb immediately continued His journey to <u>Sh</u>íráz. Free and without chains, He went before His guards, who followed Him respectfully. By the magic of His words, He had disarmed their hostility and had changed their pride and arrogance into humility and love.

Arriving in <u>Sh</u>íráz, the Báb was brought before the governor, who treated Him with shameful cruelty. He publicly rebuked and criticized the Báb. He then released Him into the custody of His uncle. Although the Báb was allowed to return to His home, His freedom was restricted. Only the members of His family and a few others were permitted to see Him. Yet, over the months that followed, in spite of attempts by the governor and the clergy to put an end to His influence, the number of His followers rapidly increased.

The fame of the Báb soon became so great that the King sent one of his most trusted and knowledgeable scholars to <u>Sh</u>íráz in order to investigate the situation. A guest in the home of the governor himself, the scholar, who would later be known as Vaḥíd, met with the Báb on three occasions. Determined each time to refute the arguments of the Báb, he grew increasingly awed by His knowledge, eloquence, and wisdom. In the third meeting Vaḥíd became utterly convinced of the Youth's divine Station. Later, referring to his meetings with the Báb, Vaḥíd explained that he felt as "lowly as the dust beneath His feet." Vaḥíd immediately sent a written report to the King's court and left <u>Sh</u>íráz at the instructions of the Báb. From that day forward, he dedicated his energies to the promotion of His Cause and eventually laid down his life in the path of his Beloved.

With the Báb's rising power and fame, the governor's anger grew and he again ordered His arrest. This time the governor intended to put the Báb to death. But, on the very night of His arrest, a plague broke out in <u>Sh</u>íráz and the entire city was thrown into a state of panic. Within a few hours, over a hundred people had died from the dreaded disease. A police official, whose son was miraculously cured by the Báb, recognized the Hand of God in the outbreak of this plague and pleaded with the governor to release the Báb. The governor, fearing for the lives of his family and the inhabitants of the city, accepted on condition that the Báb would leave <u>Sh</u>íráz.

In the fall of 1846 the Báb departed for Iṣfáhán, a city north of <u>Sh</u>íráz. As He said farewell to His uncle, He told him: "I will again meet you amid the mountains of Ádhirbáyján, from whence I will send you forth to obtain the crown of martyrdom. I Myself will follow you, together with one of My loyal disciples, and will join you in the realm of eternity." [13]

Exercises:

1.   What did Quddús do when he arrived in <u>Sh</u>íráz? _____

_____

2.   Who opposed Quddús when he began to teach the new Faith in <u>Sh</u>íráz? _____

_____

3. What does the word "clergy" mean? _____

_____

4. What words describe the character of the governor?_____

_____

5. The governor commanded that the _____ of Quddús and his companion should be _____, that their _____ be _____ with a _____ through which a _____ be _____, and that with this cord, they should be _____ through the _____ for all to see.

6. The governor then instructed his guards to _____ the Báb and to _____ Him in _____ to Shíráz.

7. What does the word "heresy" mean? _____

8. What was the Báb doing when the guards met Him?_____

_____

9. As the guards approached the Báb, He _____ them and _____ as to their _____. The leader of the guards thought it was best to hide the truth from the Báb, but He smilingly observed: "The _____ has _____ you to _____ Me. _____ am I; do with _____ as you _____. By coming out to _____ you, I have _____ the _____ of your _____, and have made it _____ for you to _____ Me." The leader tried to ignore the Báb and was preparing to leave, when the Báb said: ". . . I have _____ My own _____ and have _____ being the _____ of _____ or _____ to anyone. I _____ that you are _____ Me. I prefer to _____ _____ into your _____, rather than _____ you and your _____ to _____ for My sake."

10. How did the Báb disarm the hostility of His guards? _____

_____

11. How did the Báb arrive in Shíráz? _____

_____

12.	How did the governor treat the Báb? _____

	_____

13.	What actions did the governor take against the Báb? _____

	_____

	_____

	_____

14.	In spite of _____ by the governor and the clergy to put an end to

	the Báb's _____, the number of His _____ rapidly

	_____.

15.	Who is Vaḥíd? _____

	_____

	_____

16.	What made the governor finally release the Báb and allow Him to leave Shíráz?

	_____

17.	Where did the Báb go when He left Shíráz? _____

18.	When did He make this journey? _____

19.	What did the Báb tell His uncle when He said farewell to him? _____

	_____

	_____

	_____

	_____

20.	Pretend you are the leader of the mounted escort and, with the help of your tutor, tell the story of your encounter with the Báb to the other members of your group. You should be sure to use the necessary drama and emotion in doing so.

SECTION 5

As the Báb neared the city of Iṣfáhán, He wrote a letter to the governor of that province requesting him to appoint the place where He should live. Unlike the governor in Shíráz, this governor was a pure-hearted and just man. He was so moved by the courtesy and style of the Báb's letter that he instructed the highest religious official of the province to receive the Báb in his home and to give Him a warm and generous reception.

During the Báb's stay in Iṣfáhán, His fame gradually spread throughout the entire city. Crowds of people came to see Him every day and listen to His words of wisdom. But the Báb's growing popularity aroused the jealousy of the clergy of the city, who were afraid of losing their own position and power. They began to spread rumors about the Báb, hoping to excite suspicion against Him. When this failed, they devised a plan to do away with Him. The governor, aware of the clergy's schemes against the Báb, decided it would be best to have Him come and stay in his own home. There, during hours spent in conversation with the Báb, the governor gradually came to understand the greatness of His Revelation. One day, while seated with the Báb in the garden of his home, the governor addressed Him in these words:

> "The almighty Giver has endowed me with great riches. I know not how best to use them. Now that I have, by the aid of God, been led to recognize this Revelation, it is my ardent desire to consecrate all my possessions to the furtherance of its interests and the spread of its fame. It is my intention to proceed, by Your leave, to Ṭihrán, and to do my best to win to this Cause the King, whose confidence in me is firm and unshaken." [14]

To this outpouring of love and devotion, the Báb replied:

> "May God requite you for your noble intentions. So lofty a purpose is to Me even more precious than the act itself. Your days and Mine are numbered, however; they are too short to enable Me to witness, and allow you to achieve, the realization of your hopes. Not by the means which you fondly imagine will an almighty Providence accomplish the triumph of His Faith. Through the poor and lowly of this land, by the blood which these shall have shed in His path, will the omnipotent Sovereign ensure the preservation and consolidate the foundation of His Cause. That same God will, in the world to come, place upon your head the crown of immortal glory, and will shower upon you His inestimable blessings. Of the span of your earthly life there remain only three months and nine days, after which you shall, with faith and certitude, hasten to your eternal abode." [15]

Three months and nine days later the governor passed away, exactly as the Báb had foretold. A few days after his death, his successor sent a message to the King in Ṭihrán asking him what he should do with the Báb. The King ordered him to send the Báb in disguise to the capital, where the King intended to meet Him. Thus, in the company of a mounted escort, the Báb began His journey to Ṭihrán.

Exercises:

1.   To whom did the Báb write as He approached the city of Iṣfáhán?_____

2.   The governor of Iṣfáhán was a _____ and _____ man.

3.   What instructions did the governor give to the highest religious official of the province? _____

_____

4.   During the Báb's stay in _____, His _____ gradually _____ throughout the entire city. _____ of _____ came to _____ Him every day and _____ to His _____ of _____ .

5.   What made the clergy of Iṣfáhán jealous? _____
_____

6.   What did the governor do to protect the Báb against the schemes of the clergy?
_____

7.   One day, while seated with the Báb in the garden of his home, the governor addressed Him in these words: "The _____ has _____ me with _____. I know not how _____ to _____ them. Now that I have, by the _____ of _____, been led to _____ this _____, it is my _____ to _____ all my _____ to the _____ of its _____ and the _____ of its _____."

8.   How did the Báb respond to the governor's offer? _____
_____
_____
_____
_____
_____
_____

9.   By what means did the Báb say His Faith would spread?_____
_____

10.   What orders did the King give to the governor's successor? _____
_____
_____

SECTION 6

The Prime Minister of Persia at that time was a selfish and incompetent man. He was afraid that, if the Báb came to Ṭihrán and met the King, he would lose his own position and power. Therefore, he convinced the King to change his orders and send the Báb to the province of Ádhirbáyján in the northwest of the country.

When the Báb arrived at Tabríz, the capital of the province, He was taken to one of the main houses of the city, where He was to be confined. A detachment of soldiers guarded the entrance of the house. No one was permitted to see Him, except two of His followers. The people of the city were warned that whoever tried to meet the Báb would be thrown into prison and all his possessions would be taken away.

The Báb stayed in Tabríz for a short time and was then transferred to the fortress of Máh-Kú, situated in the mountains of Ádhirbáyján far away from large cities and towns. The people of this region belong to a different sect of Islám, one which has many disagreements with the sect that the majority of the population follows. The Prime Minister had thought that by sending the Báb to this remote and inhospitable corner of the country, His influence would diminish and His Faith would gradually be forgotten. But he did not realize that the lamp of the Religion of God had been lit and that no human hand could put out its flame. The Báb, through His majesty and loving-kindness, soon won the respect and admiration of both the official in charge of the fortress and the people of the region.

The severe discipline placed upon the Báb was gradually relaxed, and the doors of the fortress were opened to His followers, who came in increasing numbers from different parts of Persia to visit Him. During the period of His imprisonment in Máh-Kú, the Báb revealed the Persian Bayán, the most important of all His Works. In that Book, He established the laws of His Dispensation, plainly and directly announced the coming of another Revelation greater than His Own, and urged His followers to seek and find "Him Whom God would make manifest". One of His followers who lived in Máh-Kú at that time described the revelation of the Persian Bayán in these words:

> "The voice of the Báb, as He dictated the teachings and principles of His Faith, could be clearly heard by those who were dwelling at the foot of the mountain. The melody of His chanting, the rhythmic flow of the verses which streamed from His lips caught our ears and penetrated into our very souls. Mountain and valley re-echoed the majesty of His voice. Our hearts vibrated in their depths to the appeal of His utterance." [16]

When the Prime Minister learned that the Báb had won the admiration of the people of Máh-Kú and that His Faith was continuing to spread throughout the country, he issued an order for the Báb to be transferred to the fortress of Chihríq. But, there too, the people of the surrounding towns and the official of the fortress were attracted to the magnetic personality of the Báb. Even some of the most distinguished clergy of the region accepted the new Faith and left their privileged positions to join His followers.

As soon as the Prime Minister heard of the Báb's growing popularity in Chihríq, he gave orders to have Him sent immediately to Tabríz. There, the government called a meeting of the religious authorities to examine the Báb and find the most effective way to put an end to His influence. At that meeting, the clergy and government officials tried to humiliate the Báb, but were overpowered by His majesty and greatness. When asked, "Whom do you claim to be, and what is the message which you have brought?" He declared:

> **"I am, I am, I am, the Promised One! I am the One whose name you have for a thousand years invoked, at whose mention you have risen, whose advent you have longed to witness, and the hour of whose Revelation you have prayed God to hasten. Verily I say, it is incumbent upon the peoples of both the East and the West to obey My word and to pledge allegiance to My person."** [17]

A few days after that meeting, the Báb was taken back to Chihríq. His enemies had hoped that by bringing Him to Tabríz they would force Him to give up His Mission. But in the end they were convinced that, as long as the Báb remained alive, it would be impossible to stop His growing influence.

Exercises:

1. What words describe the character of the Prime Minister of Persia who exiled the Báb to Ádhirbáyján? _____

2. Why was the Prime Minister afraid for the King to meet the Báb? _____
    _____

3. What did the Prime Minister do to prevent the Báb from meeting the King? ____
    _____
    _____
    _____

4. Was the Báb a prisoner when He departed from Shíráz? _____

5. Was the Báb a prisoner when He departed from Iṣfáhán? _____

6. Was the Báb a prisoner when He arrived in Tabríz? _____

7. Why did soldiers guard the entrance of the house where the Báb stayed in Tabríz?
    _____
    _____

8. The people of the city were warned that _____ tried to meet
    the Báb would be _____ into _____ and all his
    _____ would be _____.

9. From Tabríz the Báb was transferred to the _____ of _____ .

10. The Prime Minister had thought that by _____ the Báb to so _____
    and _____ a corner of the country, His _____
    would _____ and His _____ would _____ be
    _____ .

11. How was the Prime Minister's thinking mistaken? _____
    _____

12. How did the gates of the Báb's prison in Máh-Kú come to be open to His followers?

_____

_____

_____

13. What important Book did the Báb reveal during the period of His confinement in the fortress of Máh-Kú? _____

14. What are some of the themes of the Persian Bayán? _____

_____

_____

_____

15. In the Bayán, the Báb urged His followers to _____ and _____
    " _____ Whom _____ would make _____ ".

16. What did the Prime Minister do when he heard that the Báb's Faith was continuing to spread _____

_____

17. How was the Báb's Cause affected by His transfer to Chihríq? _____

_____

18. Why was the Báb taken from Chihríq to Tabríz? _____

_____

19. What did the enemies of the Báb think they would accomplish by bringing Him to Tabríz? _____

_____

20. What questions did the authorities ask the Báb during His examination? _____

_____

21. What did the Báb declare in response to their questions? _____

_____

_____

_____

_____

SECTION 7

Referring to the Báb, 'Abdu'l-Bahá has said:

> "As for the Báb—may my soul be His sacrifice!—at a youthful age, that is to say, when He had reached the twenty-fifth year of His blessed life, He stood forth to proclaim His Cause. . . . All alone, in a way which is beyond imagination, He upheld the Cause among the Persians, who are renowned for their religious fanaticism. This illustrious Soul arose with such power that He shook the supports of the religion, of the morals, the conditions, the habits and the customs of Persia, and instituted new rules, new laws and a new religion. Though the great personages of the State, nearly all the clergy, and the public men arose to destroy and annihilate Him, He alone withstood them and moved the whole of Persia.

> "Many 'ulamá and public men, as well as other people, joyfully sacrificed their lives in His Cause, and hastened to the plain of martyrdom.

> "The government, the nation, the doctors of divinity and the great personages desired to extinguish His light, but they could not do so. At last His moon arose, His star shone forth, His foundations became firmly established, and His dawning-place became brilliant. He imparted divine education to an unenlightened multitude and produced marvelous results on the thoughts, morals, customs and condition of the Persians. He announced the glad tidings of the manifestation of the Sun of Bahá to His followers and prepared them to believe.

> "The appearance of such wonderful signs and great results; the effects produced upon the minds of the people, and upon the prevailing ideas; the establishment of the foundations of progress; and the organization of the principles of success and prosperity by a young merchant, constitute the greatest proof that He was a perfect Educator. A just person will never hesitate to believe this." [18]

Exercise:

1. Prepare and deliver a short talk on the rise of the Bábí Faith based on the above words of 'Abdu'l-Bahá and on the history you have studied up to this point.

SECTION 8

In the year 1850, a new Prime Minister of Persia, as bloodthirsty as the previous one, ordered the execution of the Báb. Again the Báb was brought from Chihríq to Tabríz. There He was confined to a cell next to a courtyard, which was to be the scene of His martyrdom.

As the Báb was being conducted to the cell, a youth forced his way through the crowd and threw himself at the feet of the Báb. "Send me not from Thee, O Master," pleaded the youth. He begged the Báb to allow him to follow Him wherever He might go. "Arise," answered the Báb, "and rest assured that you will be with Me. Tomorrow you shall witness what God has decreed."[19] The youth was immediately arrested, together with two of his companions, and was placed in the same cell in which the Báb and His secretary were confined. This young man became known as Anís.

Anís had heard of the new Message from the Báb Himself during His previous imprisonment in Tabríz and had determined to follow Him to Chihríq. So strong was the fire of the love of God burning in Anís' heart that his only desire was to sacrifice himself for his new Faith. But his stepfather, alarmed at his son's strange behavior, confined Anís to his home and kept him under strict watch. There Anís spent weeks in prayer and meditation, imploring God to allow him to attain the presence of his Beloved. Then one day, while lost in prayer, he had an extraordinary vision. He saw the Báb standing before him and calling to him. Anís threw himself at His feet. "Rejoice," the Báb said to him, "the hour is approaching when, in this very city, I shall be suspended before the eyes of the multitude and shall fall a victim to the fire of the enemy. I shall choose no one except you to share with Me the cup of martyrdom. Rest assured that this promise which I give you will be fulfilled."[20] And so Anís began to wait patiently, knowing that the day would soon arrive when he would be reunited with his Beloved. Now, at last, he had attained his Heart's Desire.

That evening the Báb was aglow with joy. He spoke with cheerfulness to Anís and the other three loyal followers confined with Him in His prison cell. "Tomorrow," He said to them, "will be the day of My martyrdom. Would that one of you might now arise and, with his own hands, end My life. I prefer to be slain by the hand of a friend rather than by that of the enemy." None of them could think of taking so precious a life, and they remained silent, tears running from their eyes. Then, suddenly, Anís sprang to his feet and said he was ready to obey whatever the Báb might command. "This same youth who has risen to comply with My wish," the Báb declared, "will, together with Me, suffer martyrdom. Him will I choose to share with Me its crown."[21]

Early the next morning, 9 July 1850, the Báb was working with His secretary when an official suddenly interrupted their conversation. "Not until I have said to him all those things that I wish to say," the Báb told the official, "can any earthly power silence Me. Though all the world be armed against Me, yet shall they be powerless to deter Me from fulfilling, to the last word, My intention."[22] But the official did not understand the significance of the Báb's words. He made no reply and instructed the secretary to follow him. The Báb was then taken from His cell to the houses of the most prominent clergy of the city of Tabríz who, without hesitation, signed the decree for His execution.

Later that morning the Báb was conducted back to the courtyard where a crowd of nearly ten thousand people had gathered to witness His execution. He was delivered into the hands of Sám Khán, the commander of the regiment of soldiers ordered to execute Him. But Sám Khán, finding himself greatly affected by the Báb's behavior, was seized with fear that his action would bring the wrath of God upon him. "I profess the Christian Faith," he explained to the Báb, "and entertain no ill will against you. If your Cause be the Cause of Truth, enable me to free myself from the obligation to shed your blood." "Follow your instructions," the Báb replied, "and if your intention be sincere, the Almighty is surely able to relieve you from your perplexity."[23]

Sám Khán ordered his men to drive an iron nail into the wall and attach two ropes to it. From these ropes, the Báb and Anís were suspended. The regiment then arranged itself in three rows, each of two hundred and fifty men. One after the other, each row opened fire. When the smoke from the seven hundred and fifty rifles cleared away, the astonished crowd saw a scene they could hardly believe. Anís was standing before them alive and unhurt, and the Báb had disappeared from sight. The bullets had only cut the ropes from which they had been suspended. A frantic search for the Báb then began. Eventually He was found seated in His cell, completing His interrupted conversation with His secretary. "I have finished my conversation," the Báb said. "Now you may proceed to fulfill your intention."[24]

Stunned by what had taken place, Sám Khán refused to allow his men to shoot again and ordered them to leave the courtyard. Another regiment had to be brought in to carry out the execution. Once more the Báb and Anís were suspended in the courtyard, and the soldiers opened fire. This time the bullets found their mark. The bodies of the Báb and Anís were completely shattered; yet their faces remained almost untouched. As the regiment was preparing to open fire, the Báb addressed these final words to the gazing multitude:

"Had you believed in Me, O wayward generation, everyone of you would have followed the example of this youth, who stood in rank above most of you, and willingly would have sacrificed himself in My path. The day will come when you will have recognized Me; that day I shall have ceased to be with you."[25]

Exercises:

1. In what city was the Báb martyred? _____

2. Who ordered the Báb's execution? _____

3. In your own words, tell the story of how the youth, Anís, came to be martyred with the Báb. _____

_____

_____

_____

_____

_____

_____

_____

_____

_____

_____

_____

_____

_____

_____

_____

_____

_____

_____

_____

4.   Why was Anís chosen by the Báb to share with Him the crown of martyrdom?

_____

_____

5.   When the official interrupted the Báb and His secretary the morning of His execution, the Báb told him: "Not until I have said to him _____ those _____ that I _____ to say, can any _____ power _____ Me."

6.   What was the name of the commander of the regiment ordered to carry out the Báb's execution? _____

7.   What did Sám Khán ask of the Báb? _____

_____

_____

8.   What did the Báb tell Sám Khán to do? _____

_____

_____

9.   How many soldiers opened fire on the Báb and His companion Anís? _____

10. What did the astonished crowd see when the smoke from the rifles cleared away?

_____

_____

_____

11. What was the Báb doing when He was found? _____

_____

12. When He was found, the Báb said: "I have _____ My _____. Now you may proceed to _____ your _____."

13. In the space below, write the final words spoken by the Báb to the crowd that had gathered to witness His execution. _____

_____
_____
_____
_____
_____
_____
_____
_____

14.   On what date did the martyrdom of the Báb take place? _July 9, 1850_

15.   How old was the Báb at the time of His martyrdom? _____30_____

SECTION 9

To engrave upon your mind and heart the events of the life of the Báb, it is suggested that you draw in the map below the route of His travels and banishments. As you do so, try to remember what occurred in each place and meditate on its significance.

SECTION 10

In these lessons you have studied the events of the life of one of the Twin Manifestations of God for this Day. During His brief life the Báb created a spiritual revolution in Persia. Thousands upon thousands of pure souls accepted His Message and began to prepare themselves for the coming of the Manifestation of God to Whom the Báb had referred as "Him Whom God shall make manifest". You know that whenever a Manifestation of God appears on earth all the forces of oppression and darkness rise against Him and try to put out the light of His Revelation. In this case, too, not only was the Báb martyred by the ignorant leaders of Persia, but thousands of His followers were put to death. The heroic lives of these early Bábís, who watered the tree of the new-born Revelation with their blood, will be a subject of your study in the coming years. Figures such as Mullá Ḥusayn, Quddús, Ṭáhirih and Vahíd will be the source of great inspiration and courage to you throughout your life as you continue to learn about the extraordinary history of the early years of the Bahá'í Era. For now, we should complete this course by reflecting on one fundamental question: How in the space of such a short time could the lives of so many thousands of people be so transformed and, from a people steeped in superstition and enslaved by corrupt leaders, such holy souls arise and perform such heroic deeds? The key to the answer can only be found in the Person of 'Alí-Muḥammad, the Báb. Therefore let us study and meditate on certain passages from the Writings of Bahá'u'lláh, 'Abdu'l-Bahá and the Guardian about that Holy Being.

In His Will and Testament, 'Abdu'l-Bahá says:

> **"This is the foundation of the belief of the people of Bahá (may my life be offered up for them): 'His Holiness, the Exalted One (the Báb), is the Manifestation of the Unity and Oneness of God and the Forerunner of the Ancient Beauty. His Holiness the Abhá Beauty (may my life be a sacrifice for His steadfast friends) is the Supreme Manifestation of God and the Dayspring of His Most Divine Essence. All others are servants unto Him and do His bidding.'"** [26]

In *God Passes By*, we read the following passage written by the Guardian:

> **"The Báb, acclaimed by Bahá'u'lláh as the 'Essence of Essences,' the 'Sea of Seas,' the 'Point round Whom the realities of the Prophets and Messengers revolve,' 'from Whom God hath caused to proceed the knowledge of all that was and shall be,' Whose 'rank excelleth that of all the Prophets,' and Whose 'Revelation transcendeth the comprehension and understanding of all their chosen ones,' had delivered His Message and discharged His mission. He Who was, in the words of 'Abdu'l-Bahá, the 'Morn of Truth' and 'Harbinger of the Most Great Light,' Whose advent at once signalized the termination of the 'Prophetic Cycle' and the inception of the 'Cycle of Fulfillment,' had simultaneously through His Revelation banished the shades of night that had descended upon His country, and proclaimed the impending rise of that Incomparable Orb Whose radiance was to envelop the whole of mankind."** [27]

Bahá'u'lláh Himself explains:

> **"That so brief a span should have separated this most mighty and wondrous Revelation from Mine own previous Manifestation, is a secret that no man can unravel and a mystery such as no mind can fathom."** [28]

'Abdu'l-Bahá says:

"The appearance of the Báb resembles the dawn, for the dawn holds the promise of the sun. The dawn of the Báb promised the rising of the Sun of Truth that is to envelop the whole world." [29]

SECTION 11

During His brief life as a Manifestation of God on earth, the Báb revealed a great number of Books and Tablets. Now that you have completed your study of His life, it is recommended that you memorize two of His prayers and at least part of His address to the Letters of the Living.

"Is there any Remover of difficulties save God? Say: Praised be God! He is God! All are His servants, and all abide by His bidding!" [30]

"Say: God sufficeth all things above all things, and nothing in the heavens or in the earth but God sufficeth. Verily, He is in Himself the Knower, the Sustainer, the Omnipotent." [31]

"O My beloved friends! You are the bearers of the name of God in this Day. You have been chosen as the repositories of His mystery. It behooves each one of you to manifest the attributes of God, and to exemplify by your deeds and words the signs of His righteousness, His power and glory. The very members of your body must bear witness to the loftiness of your purpose, the integrity of your life, the reality of your faith, and the exalted character of your devotion. For verily I say, this is the Day spoken of by God in His Book: 'On that day will We set a seal upon their mouths; yet shall their hands speak unto Us, and their feet shall bear witness to that which they shall have done.' Ponder the words of Jesus addressed to His disciples, as He sent them forth to propagate the Cause of God. In words such as these, He bade them arise and fulfill their mission: 'Ye are even as the fire which in the darkness of the night has been kindled upon the mountain-top. Let your light shine before the eyes of men. Such must be the purity of your character and the degree of your renunciation, that the people of the earth may through you recognize and be drawn closer to the heavenly Father who is the Source of purity and grace. For none has seen the Father who is in heaven. You who are His spiritual children must by your deeds exemplify His virtues, and witness to His glory. You are the salt of the earth, but if the salt have lost its savor, wherewith shall it be salted? Such must be the degree of your detachment, that into whatever city you enter to proclaim and teach the Cause of God, you should in no wise expect either meat or reward from its people. Nay, when you depart out of that city, you should shake the dust from off your feet. As you have entered it pure and undefiled, so must you depart from that city. For verily I say, the heavenly Father is ever with you and keeps watch over you. If you be faithful to Him, He will assuredly deliver into your hands all the treasures of the earth, and will exalt you above all the rulers and kings of the world.' O My Letters! Verily I say, immensely exalted is this Day above the days of the Apostles of old. Nay, immeasurable is the difference! You are the witnesses of the Dawn of the promised Day of God. You are the partakers of the mystic chalice of His Revelation. Gird up the loins of endeavor, and be mindful of the words of God as revealed in His Book: 'Lo, the Lord thy God is come, and with Him is the company of His angels arrayed before Him!' Purge your hearts of worldly desires, and let angelic virtues be your adorning. Strive that by your deeds you may bear witness to the truth of these words of God, and beware lest, by 'turning back,' He may 'change you for another people,' who 'shall not be your like,' and who shall take from you the Kingdom of God. The days when idle worship was deemed sufficient are ended. The time is come when naught but the purest motive, supported by deeds of stainless purity, can ascend to the throne of the Most High and be acceptable unto Him. 'The good word riseth up unto Him, and the righteous deed will cause it to be exalted before Him.' You are the lowly, of whom God has thus spoken in His Book: 'And We desire to show favor to those who were brought low in the land, and to make them spiritual leaders among men, and to make them Our heirs.' You have been called to this station; you will attain to it, only if you arise to trample beneath your feet every earthly desire, and endeavor to become those 'honored servants of His who speak not till He hath spoken, and who do His bidding.' You are the first Letters that have been generated from the Primal Point, the first Springs that have welled out from the Source of this Revelation. Beseech the Lord your God to grant that no earthly entanglements, no worldly affections, no ephemeral pursuits, may tarnish the purity, or embitter the sweetness, of that grace which flows through you. I am preparing you for the advent of a mighty Day. Exert your utmost endeavor that, in the world to come, I, who am now instructing you, may, before the mercy-seat of God, rejoice in your deeds and glory in your achievements. The secret of the Day that is to come is now concealed. It can neither be divulged nor estimated. The newly born babe of that Day excels the wisest and most venerable men of this time, and the lowliest and most unlearned of that period shall surpass in understanding the most erudite and accomplished divines of this age. Scatter throughout the length and breadth of this land, and, with steadfast feet and sanctified hearts, prepare the way for His coming. Heed not your weaknesses and frailty; fix your gaze upon the invincible power of the Lord, your God, the Almighty. Has He not, in past days, caused Abraham, in spite of His seeming helplessness, to triumph over the forces of Nimrod? Has He not enabled Moses, whose staff was His only companion, to vanquish Pharaoh and his hosts? Has He not established the ascendancy of Jesus, poor and lowly as He was in the eyes of men, over the combined forces of the Jewish people? Has He not subjected the barbarous and militant tribes of Arabia to the holy and transforming discipline of Muḥammad, His Prophet? Arise in His name, put your trust wholly in Him, and be assured of ultimate victory." [32]

SECTION 12

The account you have just studied of the life of the Báb will assist you in your efforts to deepen newly enrolled believers. Although at first they need not learn the story in great detail, it will be important for them to know the major events of His life and to recognize that He was the Forerunner of Bahá'u'lláh and the Herald of a New Age. You will find the pages that follow helpful on certain occasions.

The Báb

The Herald of the New Day

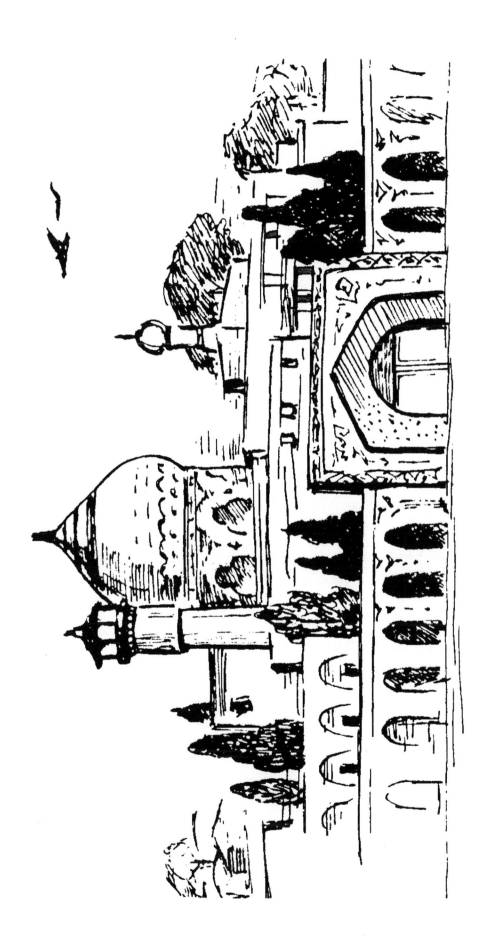

The Báb was born on 20 October 1819 in <u>Sh</u>íráz, a city in the southern part of Iran. He was still a child when His father passed away. He was raised by His uncle, who placed Him in school at an early age.

1

The Báb's teacher quickly recognized His great capacity and realized that he was incapable of teaching such an extraordinary child. The Báb was endowed by God with innate knowledge.

2

At that time the people of Iran were awaiting the coming of a new Messenger of God. They prayed that He would soon be made manifest, bringing with Him a period of peace and justice on earth. Many left their homes in search of the Promised One.

3

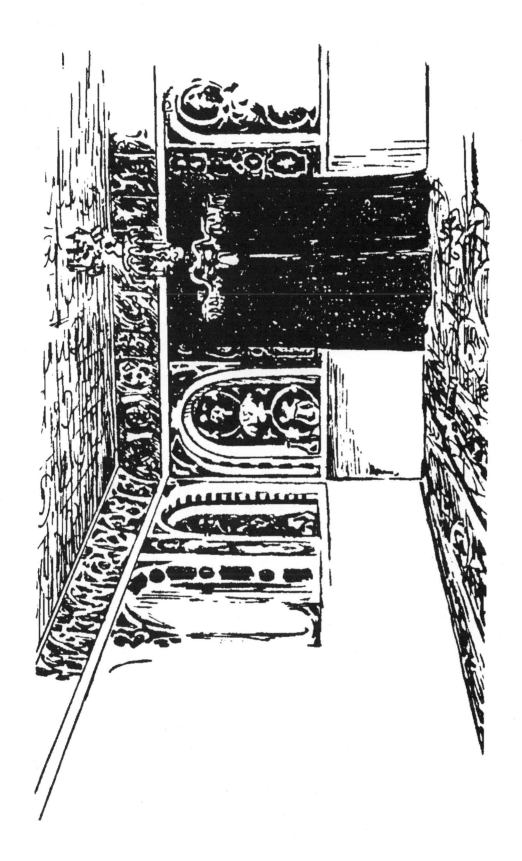

On the eve of 23 May 1844, a young man arrived in Shíráz in search of the Promised One. The Báb met him outside the gates of the city and invited him to His home to refresh himself after his long journey. There the Báb declared that He was the One Whose coming the people were so eagerly awaiting.

4

The word "Báb" means gate or door. The Báb announced that soon another Messenger of God would appear Who would unite all the peoples of the world in one family. The Báb was like a door leading humanity to a new and glorious future.

5

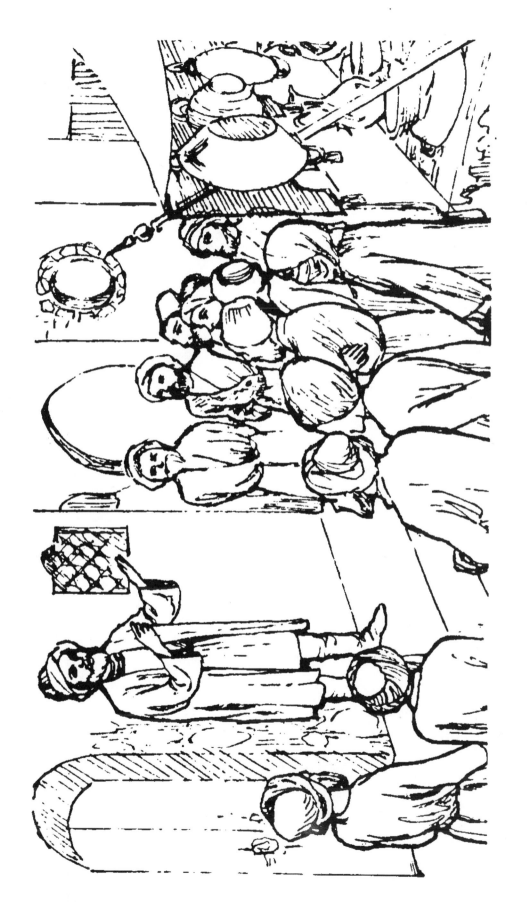

The number of the Báb's followers quickly grew. Throughout all of Iran, they began to spread the Divine Teachings revealed by Him.

6

But soon the government authorities and the clergy, who were afraid of the Truth, rose up against the new Faith of God. They imprisoned the Báb in a fortress in a remote part of the country, far away from His followers.

7

The Báb's followers suffered the most cruel persecution. They were attacked, beaten and thrown into prison. Thousands were put to death, yet the Cause of God continued to spread.

8

In the year 1850 the Báb was martyred. At the order of the government, He was suspended in a courtyard together with one of His followers and shot by a regiment of soldiers. The Báb was only 31 years old.

9

The Báb gave His life to prepare the way for the coming of Bahá'u'lláh, "The Glory of God", the banner of Whose Faith was destined to be raised in every corner of the planet.

10

REFERENCES

1. *The Dawn-Breakers: Nabíl's Narrative of the Early Days of the Bahá'í Revelation* (Wilmette: Bahá'í Publishing Trust, 1974), pp. 75-76.

2. Shoghi Effendi, *God Passes By* (Wilmette: Bahá'í Publishing Trust, 1995), p. xiv.

3. *The Dawn-Breakers*, p. 57.

4. Ibid., p. 63.

5. Ibid., p. 65.

6. *The Promulgation of Universal Peace: Talks Delivered by 'Abdu'l-Bahá during His Visit to the United States and Canada in 1912* (Wilmette: Bahá'í Publishing Trust, 1995), p. 138.

7. *The Dawn-Breakers*, pp. 85-86.

8. Ibid., pp. 92-94.

9. Ibid., pp. 142-43.

10. Ibid., p. 146.

11. *The Promulgation of Universal Peace*, p. 138.

12. *The Dawn-Breakers*, pp. 148-50.

13. Ibid., p. 198.

14. Ibid., p. 212.

15. Ibid., p. 213.

16. Ibid., p. 249.

17. Ibid., pp. 315-16.

18. *Some Answered Questions* (Wilmette: Bahá'í Publishing Trust, 1994), pp. 25-26.

19. *The Dawn-Breakers*, p. 507.

20. Ibid., pp. 307-08.

21. Ibid., p. 508.

22. Ibid., p. 509.

23.   Ibid., p. 512.

24.   Ibid., p. 513.

25.   Ibid., p. 514.

26.   *Will and Testament of 'Abdu'l-Bahá* (Wilmette: Bahá'í Publishing Trust, 1991), p. 19.

27.   *God Passes By*, p. 57.

28.   Bahá'u'lláh, cited in *The World Order of Bahá'u'lláh: Selected Letters* (Wilmette: Bahá'í Publishing Trust, 1991), p. 124.

29.   *'Abdu'l-Bahá on Divine Philosophy* (Boston: Tudor Press, 1918), pp. 47-48.

30.   The Báb, *Bahá'í Prayers: A Selection of Prayers Revealed by Bahá'u'lláh, the Báb, and 'Abdu'l-Bahá* (Wilmette: Bahá'í Publishing Trust, 1993), p. 28.

31.   The Báb, Ibid., p. 29.

32.   *The Dawn-Breakers*, pp. 92-94.

The Life of Bahá'u'lláh

Purpose

To learn to narrate the story of Bahá'u'lláh's life
and gain an appreciation of the magnitude of
the spiritual forces released by Him.

Practice

Visit a few families and share with them
a simple illustrated presentation of Bahá'u'lláh's life.

SECTION 1

Bahá'u'lláh, Whose name was Mírzá Ḥusayn-'Alí, was born on 12 November 1817 in Ṭihrán, the capital of Persia. His father, Mírzá Buzurg, was a distinguished nobleman who held a high-ranking position in the court of the Persian King. From an early age, Bahá'u'lláh showed signs of greatness and displayed extraordinary knowledge and wisdom. He did not attend regular school and only received some instruction at home. Regarding His childhood, 'Abdu'l-Bahá says:

> **"The Blessed Perfection, Bahá'u'lláh, belonged to the nobility of Persia. From earliest childhood He was distinguished among His relatives and friends. They said, 'This child has extraordinary power.' In wisdom, intelligence and as a source of new knowledge, He was advanced beyond His age and superior to His surroundings. All who knew Him were astonished at His precocity. It was usual for them to say, 'Such a child will not live,' for it is commonly believed that precocious children do not reach maturity."** [1]

In a Tablet, Bahá'u'lláh Himself tells a story from His childhood of the occasion when He attended the wedding celebration of one of His brothers in Ṭihrán. As was the custom in Ṭihrán at that time, a great feast was held for seven days and nights. On the last day, a puppet show about a famous king was performed as entertainment for the guests. Bahá'u'lláh sat in an upper room overlooking the courtyard where a tent had been set up for the performance.

He tells us that the play began with the entrance of a few small figures in human form announcing that the king was approaching. Several more figures then appeared. Some were sweeping, and others were sprinkling water in preparation for the king's arrival. Soon after, the town crier entered the scene and told the people to assemble for an audience with the king. Several groups of figures then made their appearance and took their proper places. Finally, the king made his grand entrance. Wearing a crown on his head, he walked slowly and majestically and seated himself on a throne. Shots were fired; trumpets blasted, and the tent was filled with smoke.

When the smoke cleared, the king, still seated on his throne, was seen surrounded by ministers, princes and state officials, all standing at attention in his presence. At that moment, a thief was brought before the king, who gave the order that he should be beheaded. Without delay, the chief executioner carried out his instructions. After the execution, the king fell into conversation with his ministers and officials. Suddenly news arrived that a rebellion had broken out in one of the frontiers. Troops were immediately dispatched to crush the uprising. A few minutes later, the sound of cannon shot was heard in the background, and it was announced that the king's troops were engaged in battle against the rebels.

Thus the play continued. Bahá'u'lláh was greatly puzzled by the nature of the show. After it was over and the curtain was drawn, He saw a man come out from behind the tent carrying a box under his arm. **"What is this box,"** Bahá'u'lláh asked him, **"and what was the nature of this display?"** **"All this lavish display and these elaborate devices,"** he replied, **"the king, the princes, and the ministers, their pomp and glory, their might and power, everything you saw, are all now contained within this box."** [2] This statement made a great impression on Bahá'u'lláh, and He has declared that:

"Ever since that day, all the trappings of the world have seemed in the eyes of this Youth akin to that same spectacle. They have never been, nor will they ever be, of any weight and consequence, be it to the extent of a grain of mustard seed. . . . Erelong these outward trappings, these visible treasures, these earthly vanities, these arrayed armies, these adorned vestures, these proud and overweening souls, all shall pass into the confines of the grave, as though into that box. In the eyes of those possessed of insight, all this conflict, contention and vainglory hath ever been, and will ever be, like unto the play and pastimes of children."[3]

Another story associated with Bahá'u'lláh's childhood is related to a dream that His father had in which Bahá'u'lláh appeared to be:

". . . swimming in a vast, limitless ocean. His body shone upon the waters with a radiance that illumined the sea. Around His head, which could distinctly be seen above the waters, there radiated, in all directions, His long, jet-black locks, floating in great profusion above the waves. . . . a multitude of fishes gathered round Him, each holding fast to the extremity of one hair. Fascinated by the effulgence of His face, they followed Him in whatever direction He swam. Great as was their number, and however firmly they clung to His locks, not one single hair seemed to have been detached from His head, nor did the least injury affect His person. Free and unrestrained, He moved above the waters and they all followed Him."[4]

Impressed by this dream, Bahá'u'lláh's father called a man known for his insight and asked him to interpret it for him. This man, as if inspired by a glimpse of the future glory of Bahá'u'lláh, said:

"The limitless ocean that you have seen in your dream is none other than the world of being. Single-handed and alone, your son will achieve supreme ascendancy over it. Wherever He may please, He will proceed unhindered. No one will resist His march, no one will hinder His progress. The multitude of fishes signifies the turmoil which He will arouse amidst the peoples and kindreds of the earth. Around Him will they gather, and to Him will they cling. Assured of the unfailing protection of the Almighty, this tumult will never harm His person, nor will His loneliness upon the sea of life endanger His safety."[5]

Exercises:

1. What was Bahá'u'lláh's name? _____

2. On what date was He born? _____

3. Where was He born? _____

4. By what other name is Persia known today? _____

5. What was the name of Bahá'u'lláh's father? _____

6. What kind of position did Bahá'u'lláh's father hold? _____

7.   What signs did Bahá'u'lláh display as a child? _____

_____

8.   What kind of education did Bahá'u'lláh receive? _____

_____

9.   Describe the puppet show that Bahá'u'lláh saw in His childhood. _____

_____

_____

_____

_____

_____

_____

_____

_____

_____

_____

10.   What did Bahá'u'lláh think when He learned that the play with its king, ministers,
      soldiers and throne had all been put away in a box? _____

_____

_____

_____

11.   Bahá'u'lláh has declared that from the day He saw the king, his ministers, soldiers
      and throne put away in a box: ". . . all the _____ of the
      _____ have seemed in the_____ of this _____ akin to
      that same _____. They have _____ been, nor will ever
      be, _____ of _____, though it be to the extent
      of a _____ of _____ . . . . Erelong these _____
      _____, these _____, these _____,
      these _____, this _____,
      these _____ and _____—all shall
      pass into the confines of the _____, as though into that box. In
      the eyes of those possessed of _____, all this _____,
      _____ and _____ hath been, and will ever be,
      like unto the_____ of _____."

12. Relate in your own words Mírzá Buzurg's dream. _____

_____

_____

_____

_____

_____

_____

_____

_____

13. What was the meaning of the ocean in the dream? _____

_____

14. What was the meaning of the fish? _____

_____

15. What did it mean that Bahá'u'lláh moved free and unrestrained above the waters?

_____

_____

_____

SECTION 2

The Divine Manifestations are endowed with innate knowledge and do not need to acquire learning at schools and universities. They are the educators, not the educated. Bahá'u'lláh says:

> "This Wronged One hath frequented no school, neither hath He attended the controversies of the learned. By My life! Not of Mine own volition have I revealed Myself, but God, of His own choosing, hath manifested Me."[6]

In reference to Bahá'u'lláh's innate knowledge, 'Abdu'l-Bahá says:

> "No one entered His presence without becoming awe-stricken by His might. The learned men who approached Him were astounded at His knowledge, yet He never attended school nor learned of men. His friends and His family all testify to this, yet His Teachings are the soul of this age.

> "The sun emanates from itself and does not draw its light from other sources. The Divine Teachers have the innate light; They have knowledge and understanding of all things in the universe; the rest of the world receives its light from Them and through Them the arts and sciences are revived in each age."[7]

Exercises:

1. Complete the following sentences:

   a. The sun emanates from _____; it does not draw its _____ from _____.

   b. The Divine Teachers have the _____.

   c. The Divine Teachers have _____ and_____ of all things in the universe.

   d. From the Divine Teachers, the rest of the world _____.

   e. Through the Divine Teachers, the arts and the sciences are _____ _____.

2. In your group, discuss the meaning of innate knowledge and of acquired knowledge.

3. Memorize the above quotation from the Writings of Bahá'u'lláh.

SECTION 3

As Bahá'u'lláh grew, the signs of His greatness became increasingly manifest. By the time He was a youth, He was renowned for His keen intelligence, His excellent character, His generosity and compassion. He was capable of solving the most difficult problems and of answering the most complicated and profound questions. Yet despite His extraordinary powers, He never sought position or prominence. When His father passed away, Bahá'u'lláh was asked to follow in his footsteps and assume his position in the court of the King. But He refused. He was not interested in the titles and honors of this world. His interest lay in defending the poor and protecting the needy. At the age of eighteen, Bahá'u'lláh married Ásíyih Khánum and their home became a shelter to all. No one was denied their hospitality.

Bahá'u'lláh was twenty-seven years old when, on 23 May 1844, the Báb declared His Mission to Mullá Ḥusayn in Shíráz. Scarcely three months after that historic event, Bahá'u'lláh received a scroll from the Báb which contained some of His Writings. He instantly testified to the truth of the Báb's Revelation and arose to promote His Teachings. The story of how Bahá'u'lláh came to receive that scroll is as follows.

Soon after the Báb had appointed His chosen disciples, the eighteen Letters of the Living, He called them to His presence and instructed them to spread out and teach His Faith. He gave to each one a special task, assigning to some their own native provinces as the field of their endeavors. Of these eighteen blessed souls, Quddús was chosen to accompany Him on His pilgrimage to Mecca, where He was to proclaim His Mission. To Mullá Ḥusayn, the first to believe in Him, He addressed these words: "Grieve not that you have not been chosen to accompany Me on My Pilgrimage to Ḥijáz. I shall, instead, direct your steps to that city which enshrines a Mystery of such transcendent holiness as neither Ḥijáz nor S̲h̲íráz can hope to rival." [8] He gave Mullá Ḥusayn a scroll and instructed him to proceed to Ṭihrán. He told him to beseech God that He would enable him to recognize the splendor of the secret hidden in that city and enter the presence of the Beloved.

Mullá Ḥusayn set out on his mission and, after passing through several cities, arrived in Ṭihrán. There he took a room in a school for religious studies. One of his first acts was to proclaim the Báb's Message to the head of that school, who rejected it with arrogance. However, a young student of the school overheard their conversation and was deeply affected by the words of Mullá Ḥusayn. He decided to visit him at the hour of midnight and learn more about the Message he proclaimed with such enthusiasm. Mullá Ḥusayn received the young man and spoke to him with great courtesy and kindness. He told him that he now understood why he had come to this place. The head of the school had disdainly rejected the Message he had brought. "My hope," said Mullá Ḥusayn, "is that his pupil may, unlike his master, recognize its truth." [9]

During their conversation, Mullá Ḥusayn asked the student where he was from. He replied that he was from the district of Núr, in the province of Mázindarán. "Tell me," inquired Mullá Ḥusayn, "is there today among the family of the late Mírzá Buzurg-i-Núrí, who was so renowned for his character, his charm, and artistic and intellectual attainments, anyone who has proved himself capable of maintaining the high traditions of that illustrious house?" [10]

"Yea," he replied "among his sons now living, one has distinguished Himself by the very traits which characterized His father. By His virtuous life, His high attainments, His loving-kindness and liberality, He has proved Himself a noble descendant of a noble father." "What is His occupation?" asked Mullá Ḥusayn. "He cheers the disconsolate and feeds the hungry." "What of His rank and position?" "He has none apart from befriending the poor and the stranger." "What is His name?" "Ḥusayn-'Alí." [11]

With each answer, Mullá Ḥusayn became more filled with delight. "How does He spend His time?" he further asked. "He roams the woods and delights in the beauties of the countryside." "What is His age?" "Eight and twenty." Mullá Ḥusayn's face was beaming with satisfaction and joy when he asked the young man: "I presume you often meet Him?" "I frequently visit His home," he responded. "Will you deliver into His hands a trust from me?" "Most assuredly," was his reply. Mullá Ḥusayn then handed him the scroll wrapped in a piece of cloth and requested him to present it to Bahá'u'lláh the next day at dawn. "Should He deign to answer me," Mullá Ḥusayn added, "will you be kind enough to acquaint me with His reply?" [12] The student took the scroll and, at daybreak, arose to carry out Mullá Ḥusayn's request.

As he neared the house of Bahá'u'lláh, he saw His brother, Mírzá Músá, standing at the gate and explained to him the reason for his visit. Mírzá Músá conducted the young man into the presence of Bahá'u'lláh, and the scroll was laid before Him. Bahá'u'lláh asked them to be seated. Unfolding the scroll, He began to read aloud some of its passages. He had read but a page when He turned to His brother and said: "Músá, what have you to say? Verily I say, whoso believes in the Qur'án and recognizes its Divine origin, and yet hesitates, though it be for a moment, to admit that these soul-stirring words are endowed with the same regenerating power, has most assuredly erred in his judgment and has strayed far from the path of justice." [13] Dismissing the young man from His presence,

Bahá'u'lláh requested him to take to Mullá Ḥusayn, as a gift from Him, a loaf of sugar and a package of tea, and to convey to him His appreciation and love.

Filled with happiness, the young man arose and hurried back to Mullá Ḥusayn. He delivered to him the gift and message from Bahá'u'lláh. No words can describe the joy with which Mullá Ḥusayn received them. With a bowed head, he accepted the gift and fervently kissed it. He then hugged the young man, kissed his eyes, and said: "My dearly beloved friend! I pray that even as you have rejoiced my heart, God may grant you eternal felicity and fill your heart with imperishable gladness." [14] The young man was greatly puzzled by Mullá Ḥusayn's behavior. What could be, he wondered, the nature of the bond that unites these two souls? What could be the cause of fellowship between them? Why should Mullá Ḥusayn have shown such happiness upon receiving so small a gift from Bahá'u'lláh? The young man was faced with a mystery that he could not unravel.

A few days later, Mullá Ḥusayn left for <u>Kh</u>urásán, a province in the northeast of Iran. As he said farewell to the young student from Núr, he told him: "Breathe not to anyone what you have heard and witnessed. Let this be a secret hidden within your breast. Divulge not His name, for they who envy His position will arise to harm Him. In your moments of meditation, pray that the Almighty may protect Him, that, through Him, He may exalt the downtrodden, enrich the poor, and redeem the fallen. The secret of things is concealed from our eyes. Ours is the duty to raise the call of the New Day and to proclaim this Divine Message unto all the people. Many a soul will, in this city, shed his blood in this path. That blood will water the Tree of God, will cause it to flourish, and to overshadow all mankind." [15]

Exercises:

1.   What did the Báb do after appointing the eighteen Letters of the Living? _____

_____

2.   Whom did the Báb choose to accompany Him on pilgrimage to Mecca? _____

3.   To what country does Ḥijáz refer? _____

4.   To Mullá Ḥusayn, the first to believe in Him, the Báb addressed these words:
     "_____ not that you have not been chosen to accompany Me on My
     _____ to _____. I shall, instead, direct your steps
     to that city which enshrines a _____ of such _____
     holiness as neither _____ nor _____ can hope to _____ ."

5.   What did the Báb give to Mullá Ḥusayn? _____

6.   Upon arriving to Ṭihrán, Mullá Ḥusayn took a room in a school for religious stud-
     ies. How did the head of that school respond to the Báb's Message? _____

_____

7.   Why had God led Mullá Ḥusayn to the school? _____

_____

8.   Where was the student who responded to the Báb's Message from? _____

_____

9.   Where was Bahá'u'lláh's ancestral home? _____

10.   For what was His father renowned? _____

_____

11.   What was Bahá'u'lláh's occupation? _____

_____

12.   What was His rank and position? _____

_____

13.   How did He spend His time? _____

_____

14.   What was His age at the time? _____

15.   What did Mullá Ḥusayn ask the student from Núr to do? _____

_____

16.   After reading a page of the scroll sent by the Báb, Bahá'u'lláh said: "Verily I
       say, whoso believes in the _____ and recognizes its _____
       _____, and yet _____, though it be for a
       _____, to admit that these soul-stirring _____ are endowed
       with the same _____, has most assuredly
       _____ in his _____ and has _____ far from the
       path of _____."

17.   How did Mullá Ḥusayn receive the gift from Bahá'u'lláh? _____

_____

18.   Relate in your own words what Mullá Ḥusayn told the student from Núr when he
       said farewell to him. _____

_____

_____

_____

_____

_____

_____

_____

_____

_____

_____

_____

19. Divide into pairs and prepare a short skit based on the above story to present to the rest of the group. The skit should consist of two scenes: 1) when the student visits Mullá Ḥusayn at midnight and 2) when he brings him the gift and message from Bahá'u'lláh the next day. Remember that the skit should have only these two scenes in which Mullá Ḥusayn and the student appear. The student's visit to Bahá'u'lláh should not be dramatized. We should never portray a Manifestation of God on stage, as to do so would be disrespectful and irreverent.

SECTION 4

The Báb referred to Bahá'u'lláh as "Him Whom God shall make manifest". The Báb's Writings, including His most Holy Book, the Bayán, contain innumerable references in praise of Him Whom God shall make manifest. Below are only a few quotations from the Writings of the Báb to give you a glimpse of the Station of Bahá'u'lláh and the relationship between the Twin Manifestations.

> **"And know thou of a certainty that by Paradise is meant recognition of and submission unto Him Whom God shall make manifest, and by the fire, the company of such souls as would fail to submit unto Him or to be resigned to His good-pleasure."** [16]

> **". . . purge thou thine ear that thou mayest hear no mention besides God, and purge thine eye that it behold naught except God, and thy conscience that it perceive naught other than God, and thy tongue that it proclaim nothing but God, and thy hand to write naught but the words of God, and thy knowledge that it comprehend naught except God, and thy heart that it entertain no wish save God, and in like manner purge all thine acts and thy pursuits that thou mayest be nurtured in the paradise of pure love, and perchance mayest attain the presence of Him Whom God shall make manifest, adorned with a purity which He highly cherisheth, and be sanctified from whosoever hath turned away from Him and doth not support Him."** [17]

> **"Say, verily, the good-pleasure of Him Whom God shall make manifest is the good-pleasure of God, while the displeasure of Him Whom God shall make manifest is none other than the displeasure of God."** [18]

Exercises:

1.   To Whom does "Him Whom God shall make manifest" refer? _____

2.   The Báb urges His followers to prepare themselves so that they will be accepted into the presence of Him Whom God shall make manifest. What does He tell them to do?

_____

_____

_____

_____

_____

_____

3.   Choose one of the above quotations and memorize it.

SECTION 5

From the moment Bahá'u'lláh testified to the truth of the Báb's Revelation, He arose to proclaim it. The first journey He undertook to teach the new Faith was to His ancestral home in Núr, in the province of Mázindarán. There He went to His family home in the village of Tákur.

The news of Bahá'u'lláh's arrival in Tákur traveled fast throughout the region. Many of the local officials and dignitaries came to greet Him and, at the same time, learn from Him news about the King, his court and the affairs of state. But Bahá'u'lláh responded to their inquiries with little interest. He would quickly change the subject and begin to set forth, in the most eloquent manner, the Message proclaimed by the Báb. His words were so convincing and His arguments so sound that all were amazed. Those who heard Him were surprised that a person of His high position would take such a keen interest in matters which usually concerned the clergy and religious leaders. His enthusiasm and depth of knowledge soon attracted large numbers to the new Faith, including many prominent individuals and members of His own family. No one who entered His presence could escape the flow of His sweet words or dared to oppose the truth of His statements, no one except His own uncle.

This uncle did everything possible to discredit Bahá'u'lláh and the truth of the Message He had brought. But when he realized he was incapable of doing so, he went to a well-known Muslim clergyman and pleaded for his assistance. He complained that Bahá'u'lláh had come to Núr and, although not of the clergy, was speaking on religious matters. He warned the theologian that everyone who entered Bahá'u'lláh's presence fell under His spell and was overtaken by the power of His words. "I know not whether he is a sorcerer," he said, "or whether he mixes with his tea some mysterious substance that makes every man who drinks the tea fall a victim to its charm." [19]

Knowing that he could never succeed in challenging Bahá'u'lláh, the theologian ignored the pleas of the uncle. But the Message of the Báb continued to spread like wildfire throughout the district. Alarmed, the followers of the theologian began to put pressure on him to take some form of action, and finally he decided to send his two most outstanding pupils to visit Bahá'u'lláh and investigate the nature of the Message He was propagating. This is the story of what happened when those two representatives entered the presence of Bahá'u'lláh.

On being told, upon their arrival in Tákur, that Bahá'u'lláh had left for His winter home, the representatives of the theologian decided to follow Him there. When they arrived, they found Bahá'u'lláh engaged in revealing a commentary on one of the chapters of the Qur'án. As they sat and listened to Him, they were profoundly impressed by the eloquence of His presentation and the extraordinary manner in which He spoke. One of the representatives, unable to contain himself, arose from his seat and walked to the back of the room and, in an attitude of respect and submissiveness, stood still beside the door. Trembling and with eyes full of tears, he told his companion: "I am powerless to question Bahá'u'lláh. The questions I had planned to ask Him have vanished suddenly from my memory. You are free either to proceed with your inquiry or to return alone to our teacher and inform him of the state in which I find myself. Tell him from me that I can never again return to him. I can no longer forsake this threshold." But the other representative was equally struck by Bahá'u'lláh's words and followed the example of his friend. "I have ceased to recognize my teacher," was his reply. "This very moment, I have vowed to God to dedicate the remaining days of my life to the service of Bahá'u'lláh, my true and only Master."[20]

The news of the conversion of the theologian's pupils spread rapidly among the population of Núr. Dignitaries, state officials, religious leaders, traders and peasants crowded to the presence of Bahá'u'lláh. Hundreds were brought under the banner of the new Faith. No one except Bahá'u'lláh knew, however, that a terrible persecution was soon to follow, a persecution that would tear out by their very roots many of these newly born and tender plants.

Exercises:

1. What did Bahá'u'lláh do after testifying to the truth of the Báb's Revelation?___

    _____

2. How was Bahá'u'lláh received by the inhabitants of Núr?_____

    _____

3. Why were some people surprised by the way Bahá'u'lláh answered their questions?

    _____

    _____

4. What did the uncle of Bahá'u'lláh do when He began to proclaim the Cause of the Báb? _____

    _____

    _____

    _____

5. Why did the theologian ignore the uncle's pleas? _____

_____

6. What did the theologian finally decide to do when faced with pressure from his followers? _____

_____

7. Relate in your own words the story of the theologian's two representatives who entered the presence of Bahá'u'lláh. _____

_____

_____

_____

_____

_____

_____

_____

_____

_____

_____

_____

_____

_____

_____

_____

_____

_____

8. What effect did the conversion of these two representatives have on the progress of the Cause of the Báb in Mázindarán? _____

_____

_____

_____

_____

_____

SECTION 6

What Bahá'u'lláh did in the district of Núr is that which He asks us to do, to arise and teach the Cause of God. Let us, then, study and meditate on the following words of

Bahá'u'lláh, remembering that after He accepted the Báb's Revelation, His own first act was to arise and teach hundreds and hundreds of souls.

"O wayfarer in the path of God! Take thou thy portion of the ocean of His grace, and deprive not thyself of the things that lie hidden in its depths. Be thou of them that have partaken of its treasures. A dewdrop out of this ocean would, if shed upon all that are in the heavens and on the earth, suffice to enrich them with the bounty of God, the Almighty, the All-Knowing, the All-Wise. With the hands of renunciation draw forth from its life-giving waters, and sprinkle therewith all created things, that they may be cleansed from all man-made limitations and may approach the mighty seat of God, this hallowed and resplendent Spot.

"Be not grieved if thou performest it thyself alone. Let God be all-sufficient for thee. Commune intimately with His Spirit, and be thou of the thankful. Proclaim the Cause of thy Lord unto all who are in the heavens and on the earth. Should any man respond to thy call, lay bare before him the pearls of the wisdom of the Lord, thy God, which His Spirit hath sent down unto thee, and be thou of them that truly believe. And should any one reject thine offer, turn thou away from him, and put thy trust and confidence in the Lord, thy God, the Lord of all worlds." [21]

Exercises:

1. Bahá'u'lláh asks us to take our portion _____
    _____ .

2. We should not deprive ourselves of _____
    _____ .

3. A dew drop of the ocean of His grace would, if shed upon all that are in the heavens and on the earth, suffice to _____
    _____ .

4. We are asked to draw forth _____
    and sprinkle _____ .

5. We should not be grieved if _____ .

6. We should commune _____
    and be _____ .

7. We should proclaim _____
    _____ .

8.   If any man responds to our call, Bahá'u'lláh tells us to _____

_____

_____ .

9.   If any man rejects our offer, we should _____

_____

_____ .

SECTION 7

Divine Revelation is progressive. God reveals His Will progressively through His Manifestations who come from time to time as humanity advances from one stage to another. The same is true of the Revelation of each Manifestation. His Teachings are revealed gradually as the understanding of His followers increases. Oftentimes, even His closest disciples are at first incapable of grasping the full significance of His Revelation. They continue to hold on to the laws and Teachings of the previous religion. Only with time do they come to understand that the new Manifestation is changing some of the laws of the One who came before Him. His purpose is to lay down new laws for humanity's next stage of evolution.

This was the case with the Revelation of the Báb. The Muslims, among whom the Báb appeared, believed that not even a "letter" from the Teachings of the Prophet Muḥammad could be changed until the end of the world. Therefore, the Báb allowed His full Message to be made known only gradually. Initially, His sublime Station as the Promised One was not to be openly revealed. His disciples were instructed to spread the glad tidings that the Gate to the Promised One had been opened. Little by little, the person of the Báb became known, but the majority of people were still unaware of His true Station.

During the first years of His Ministry, no changes to the laws of Islám were made. In fact, this was unthinkable to even the closest of His followers. But, as you know, towards the end of His Ministry, while imprisoned in the fortress of Máh-Kú, the Báb revealed a new set of laws in the Persian Bayán. Now was the time for His followers to make a definite break with the past and to proclaim His true Station. This was done at the Conference of Badasht.

Badasht is a village some distance from Ṭihrán in the northeast part of the country. The Conference of Badasht was held in July 1848. Eighty-one of the Báb's most distinguished followers came together in this Conference. The principal participants were Bahá'u'lláh, Quddús and Ṭáhirih.

Although at first Bahá'u'lláh did not appear to have any rank among the Báb's disciples, His role at the Conference was decisive. He rented the gardens in which the Conference was held, and for twenty-two days, all those who had gathered enjoyed His generous hospitality. Each day Bahá'u'lláh revealed a Tablet to be read before the assembled believers. To each He gave a new name. To Ṭáhirih and Quddús He gave the titles by which they will be known throughout history. The title Ṭáhirih means "the Pure

One", and Quddús means "Holy". He Himself was, from that time forward, to be known by the name of Bahá. Later the Báb would reveal a special Tablet for each one of those who had attended the Conference, addressing them by the names they had received on that occasion.

One day Bahá'u'lláh was confined to His bed with illness, and the friends were gathered in His presence. Then, all of a sudden, Ṭáhirih, who was considered the essence of purity and chastity, appeared before them without the veil that, according to the beliefs of Muslims in Iran, all women had to wear in public. Some of the Bábís present felt that she had brought shame to herself and the new Faith. Quddús was visibly angry. But Ṭáhirih, unshaken and aglow with joy, addressed her companions with eloquence. She called on them to break with the past—with its religious dogmas, its traditions and ceremonies. The tension that arose between Quddús and Ṭáhirih was eased through Bahá'u'lláh's intervention. While a few of the Báb's followers left the Faith as a result of this proclamation, the majority remained firm and were filled with new enthusiasm. Bahá'u'lláh had masterfully used the occasion to celebrate the dawn of a new Day. Ṭáhirih, through her bold act, had sounded the trumpet-blast announcing the end of the old and the beginning of a new Faith.

The Conference of Badasht also marked the beginning of the most turbulent stage in the development of the Bábí Faith. Soon the persecution of its followers would reach new levels of intensity, and many would be called to martyrdom. It was as if the Conference were a farewell gathering, from where they would go out to perform deeds of great heroism, only to be reunited in the Abhá Kingdom.

Those present at the Conference departed together for Mázindarán, but were attacked along the way by the ignorant inhabitants of a village near which the group had stopped to rest. The believers were forced to flee and scattered in different directions. Bahá'u'lláh continued on to Núr in Mázindarán.

News of the Conference of Badasht soon reached Ṭihrán, and the King and his ministers became aware of the events that had taken place and the role played by Bahá'u'lláh at the Conference. The King, weak from an illness that would soon take his life, was advised by the Prime Minister to order the arrest of Bahá'u'lláh. Accordingly, an order was sent to one of the officials of Mázindarán, instructing him to arrest Bahá'u'lláh and bring Him to the capital. As it happened, the order arrived one day before that very official was to give a reception for Bahá'u'lláh, to whom he was devotedly attached. He was greatly distressed and chose not to tell anyone. The next day news reached Mázindarán that the King had died; the arrest order was no longer valid.

Exercises:

1.   What was the purpose of the Conference of Badasht?_____

       _____

2.   When did the Conference of Badasht take place? _____

3.   How many days did it last? _____

4.   How many of the Báb's followers attended the Conference? _____

5.   Who were the principal participants? _____

6.   What was proclaimed during that Conference? _____

7.   Who was the most important Figure among those present? _____

8.   What does the title "Ṭáhirih" mean? _____

9.   What does the title "Quddús" mean? _____

10. In your own words, recount the events which took place at the Conference the day
     Ṭáhirih appeared unveiled. _____

     _____

     _____

     _____

     _____

     _____

     _____

     _____

     _____

     _____

     _____

11. What did Ṭáhirih's bold act at the Conference signalize? _____

     _____

12. What did the government do when it received news of the gathering in Badasht?

     _____

13. Explain what happened after the government issued the arrest order for Bahá'u'lláh.

     _____

     _____

     _____

     _____

     _____

     _____

     _____

     _____

SECTION 8

The Conference of Bada<u>sh</u>t marked the shedding of the old and the taking up of the new. The following passage from the Writings of 'Abdu'l-Bahá describes how, from time to time down the ages, the religion of God must be renewed. Reflect on the meaning of the passage in the light of what you have studied about the Conference of Bada<u>sh</u>t.

"From the seed of reality religion has grown into a tree which has put forth leaves and branches, blossoms and fruit. After a time this tree has fallen into a condition of decay. The leaves and blossoms have withered and perished; the tree has become stricken and fruitless. It is not reasonable that man should hold to the old tree, claiming that its life forces are undiminished, its fruit unequalled, its existence eternal. The seed of reality must be sown again in human hearts in order that a new tree may grow therefrom and new divine fruits refresh the world. By this means the nations and peoples now divergent in religion will be brought into unity, imitations will be forsaken, and a universal brotherhood in reality itself will be established. Warfare and strife will cease among mankind; all will be reconciled as servants of God. For all are sheltered beneath the tree of His providence and mercy. God is kind to all; He is the giver of bounty to all alike, even as Jesus Christ has declared that God 'sendeth rain on the just and on the unjust'—that is to say, the mercy of God is universal. All humanity is under the protection of His love and favor, and unto all He has pointed the way of guidance and progress." [22]

SECTION 9

Náṣiri'd-Dín <u>Sh</u>áh, the King who rose to the throne in 1848, was far more ruthless than his father, the previous King. From the beginning of his reign, the persecutions of the Bábís increased dramatically. The Báb Himself was martyred in July of 1850 in Tabríz. His oppressed followers, who had witnessed the tragic death of thousands of their fellow believers, had now lost the most Beloved of their hearts. In their thoughts, many blamed the King for the cruelties heaped upon them over the years. But despite these feelings, they continued to be the well-wishers of the government and the people. Their energies were bent on spreading the new Faith through the power of good deeds and convincing arguments. There was, however, a small group, driven by intense anger, who were toying with dangerous ideas. In a state of despair, these foolish few believed that they could change the lot of the Bábí community by attacking tyranny at its root. They began to plot the assassination of the King.

The intentions of the group were communicated to Bahá'u'lláh by one of its leaders. Bahá'u'lláh advised him in the clearest terms that they should give up their plan. He warned them that such an act would bring fresh disasters to the already grief-stricken followers of the Báb. But the plotters were in such a state of bitterness, and the fire of vengeance burned so forcefully in their hearts, that not even the counsels of Bahá'u'lláh were able to stop them. They proceeded to commit an act that forever will be considered a stain on the pages of Bábí history, otherwise adorned with nothing but pure, selfless, and heroic deeds.

On 15 August 1852, the King left his summer residence near Ṭihrán on horseback to go for his morning ride. His personal guard moved a few steps ahead of him. There was calmness in the air; all was well for his Majesty. Then, catching everyone by surprise, a young man waiting on the roadside, pretending to be a bystander with a petition to submit to the King, attempted to slay him. So foolish was this would-be assassin that the pistol he used was charged with shot that was totally inadequate for the purpose intended. The King was wounded only slightly, but the rage that the attempt on his life created gave the enemies of the Faith an opportunity to excite the people to unimaginable acts of cruelty against the Bábís.

This ill-fated youth was immediately killed; his body was tied to the tail of a mule and dragged all the way to Ṭihrán, where it was cut into two halves and hung for the public to view. Molten lead was poured down the throat of his accomplice—this only after he had first been tortured mercilessly, yet had refused to give up the names of any of his friends. His comrade was stripped of his clothes, had lighted candles placed into holes made in his flesh, and was paraded before the crowds who shouted and cursed him.

What followed cannot be described in words. The government, the clergy, and their ignorant supporters arose to exterminate the Bábís. The gates to the city were closed, and no one was allowed to leave without being questioned. The Bábís were sought from house to house, arrested and put to death with unmatched cruelty. The following few lines from a letter written by an Austrian officer who was in the King's service give us a glimpse of the horrors of those days. Although reading his words fills us with profound sadness, we do so to be reminded of the sacrifices of the heroic souls who have watered the tree of this Cause with their blood.

"Follow me, my friend, you who lay claim to a heart and European ethics, follow me to the unhappy ones who, with gouged-out eyes, must eat, on the scene of the deed, without any sauce, their own amputated ears; or whose teeth are torn out with inhuman violence by the hand of the executioner; or whose bare skulls are simply crushed by blows from a hammer; or where the bazaar is illuminated with unhappy victims, because on right and left the people dig deep holes in their breasts and shoulders, and insert burning wicks in the wounds. I saw some dragged in chains through the bazaar, preceded by a military band, in whom these wicks had burned so deep that now the fat flickered convulsively in the wound like a newly extinguished lamp. Not seldom it happens that the unwearying ingenuity of the Oriental leads to fresh tortures. They will skin the soles of the Bábí's feet, soak the wounds in boiling oil, shoe the foot like the hoof of a horse, and compel the victim to run. No cry escaped from the victim's breast; the torment is endured in dark silence by the numbed sensation of the fanatic; now he must run; the body cannot endure what the soul has endured; he falls. Give him the *coup de grâce*! Put him out of his pain! No! The executioner swings the whip, and—I myself have had to witness it—the unhappy victim of hundredfold tortures runs! This is the beginning of the end. As for the end itself, they hang the scorched and perforated bodies by their hands and feet to a tree head downwards, and now every Persian may try his marksmanship to his heart's content from a fixed but not too proximate distance on the noble quarry placed at his disposal. I saw corpses torn by nearly one hundred and fifty bullets. . . . When I read over again what I have written I am overcome by the thought that those who are with you in our dearly beloved Austria may doubt the full truth of the picture, and accuse me of exaggeration. Would to God that I had not lived to see it! But by the duties of my profession I was unhappily often, only too often, a witness of these abominations. At present I never leave my house, in order not to meet with fresh scenes of horror . . . Since my whole soul revolts against such infamy . . . I will no longer maintain my connection with the scene of such crimes." [23]

On the day that the attempt on the life of the King took place, Bahá'u'lláh was the guest of the Prime Minister's brother in a village near Ṭihrán. The news of the calamity soon reached Him, and He was advised to hide until the storm had passed. The mother of the King blamed Bahá'u'lláh for the attempt on her son's life and was demanding His arrest. But Bahá'u'lláh refused to go into hiding; on the contrary, the next day, He mounted His horse and rode towards the headquarters of the King. The King and his court were astonished to learn of Bahá'u'lláh's approach. How could someone who was being accused of such a terrible crime, far from running away, ride so confidently towards danger? The King immediately ordered Bahá'u'lláh's arrest. The efforts of some of His friends who tried to find a refuge for Him in the house of the Prime Minister failed. He was arrested in the village of Shimírán, some 30 kilometers from the capital, and put in chains.

On foot and exposed to the fierce rays of the midsummer sun, Bahá'u'lláh was brought from Shimírán to Ṭihrán. The crowds, who had been told He was the enemy of their King, shouted abuses at Him all along the route. The story of the old woman who wished to throw a stone at Him as He approached the dungeon which was to be the place of His imprisonment captures the madness of the crowd on that day and demonstrates the love that was in His heart as He faced the most grievous of calamities.

As He was nearing that dungeon, an old and feeble woman was seen forcing her way through the crowd with a stone in her hand, eager to throw it in the face of Bahá'u'lláh. She had a look of determination and fanaticism which few women her age could muster. Her whole body shook with rage as she stepped forward and raised her hand preparing to cast her stone. "I adjure you," she pleaded, as she ran after those conducting Bahá'u'lláh to the dungeon, "give me a chance to fling my stone in his face!" "Suffer not this woman to be disappointed," were Bahá'u'lláh's words to His guards, as He saw her rushing towards Him. "Deny her not what she regards as a meritorious act in the sight of God." [24]

Exercises:

1.   What was the name of the King who rose to the throne in Persia in 1848? _____
       _____

2.   From the beginning of the reign of Náṣiri'd-Dín Sháh, the persecutions of the Bábís
       _____ .

3.   How did the Bábís in general feel after the martyrdom of the Báb? _____
       _____

4.   What was the state of mind of the group of Bábís who decided to assassinate the
       King?_____

5.   What did Bahá'u'lláh tell the leader of the group when He learned of their intentions?

_____

_____

_____

6.   On what date did the attempt on the King's life take place? _____

7.   What was the fate of those who attempted the assassination? _____

_____

_____

_____

_____

_____

_____

_____

_____

8.   What consequences did the attempted assassination have on the Bábí community?

_____

_____

_____

_____

9.   Where was Bahá'u'lláh when He learned of the attempt on the King's life?_____

_____

10. What did Bahá'u'lláh do upon receiving the news of the attempted assassination?

_____

11. In what village was Bahá'u'lláh arrested?_____

12. Since Bahá'u'lláh was not powerless before His enemies, then why do you think He allowed Himself to be arrested, knowing the danger in which He would put Himself?

_____

_____

13. Under what conditions was Bahá'u'lláh brought from Shimírán to Ṭihrán? _____

_____

_____

14.   In your own words, tell the story of the old woman who wanted to throw a stone at Bahá'u'lláh as He was being conducted to the dungeon by His guards. What does this story demonstrate? _____

_____

_____

_____

_____

_____

_____

_____

_____

_____

_____

_____

_____

_____

_____

SECTION 10

Throughout His life, Bahá'u'lláh was surrounded by enemies seeking to harm Him. But never did He try to conceal Himself; never did He protect Himself. On the contrary, at all times He was visible before the eyes of men and withstood with serenity and calm the attacks of those who opposed Him. Although they were determined to extinguish His light, they were unable to do so, and day by day His splendor grew more radiant.

> **"Not even for a single moment hath this Wronged One ever concealed Himself. Rather hath He at all times remained steadfast and conspicuous before the eyes of all men. Never have We retreated, nor shall We ever seek flight. In truth it is the foolish people who flee from Our presence. . . . Praise be to God! The Cause whereof this Wronged One is the Bearer standeth as high as heaven and shineth resplendent as the sun. Concealment hath no access unto this station, nor is there any occasion for fear or silence."** [25]

> **"Unveiled and unconcealed, this Wronged One hath, at all times, proclaimed before the face of all the peoples of the world that which will serve as the key for unlocking the doors of sciences, of arts, of knowledge, of well-being, of prosperity and wealth. Neither have the wrongs inflicted by the oppressors succeeded in silencing the shrill voice of the Most Exalted Pen, nor have the doubts of the perverse or of the seditious been able to hinder Him from revealing the Most Sublime Word."** [26]

Exercise:

1.   Describe in your own words how we, the Bahá'ís, should act in the face of difficulty.

_____

_____

_____

_____

_____

_____

_____

SECTION 11

Síyáh-Chál, the name of the prison to which Bahá'u'lláh was taken on that calamitous day, means the "Black Pit". Originally a reservoir of water for one of the public baths in Ṭihrán, it was at that time an underground dungeon in which criminals of the worst type were confined.

To reach the prison, one was taken through a pitch-black passageway and then down three steep flights of stairs. The dungeon was wrapped in thick darkness. There were no windows or outlets, other than the passage through which one entered. Nearly one hundred and fifty prisoners—thieves, murderers and highwaymen—were crowded into this dark, icy-cold space. The floor was covered with dirt and filth and crawling with insects. Most of the prisoners did not have clothes or even a cover to lie on. The smell was foul beyond belief.

Under these cruel conditions Bahá'u'lláh and a number of Bábís were imprisoned by the King. Bahá'u'lláh's feet were put in stocks, and a heavy chain weighing some 50 kilograms was placed around His neck. For the first three days and nights they were given nothing to eat or drink. The family of Bahá'u'lláh would prepare food for Him and ask the guards to bring it to Him. Although at first they refused, they gradually gave in to their pleas. But, even then, no one could be sure whether the food reached Him, or whether He would accept to eat it while His fellow-prisoners went hungry.

Bahá'u'lláh and His companions, also in stocks and chains, all huddled together in one cell. They had been placed in two rows, each facing the other. Bahá'u'lláh taught them to repeat certain verses which, every night, they chanted with great fervor. "God is sufficient unto me; He verily is the All-sufficing," one row would chant, and the other would reply: "In Him let the trusting trust." Into the early hours of the morning, the chorus of their happy voices could be heard. So strong was their melody that it reached the ears of the King, whose palace was not far from the Síyáh-Chál. "What means this sound?" he was reported to have asked. "It is the anthem the Bábís are intoning in their prison," [27] was the reply. The King fell silent.

Every day, the jailors would enter the cell and would call out the name of one of the Bábís, ordering him to arise and follow them to the foot of the gallows. With eagerness, the owner of the name would respond to that call. His chains removed, he would jump to his feet and, in a state of uncontrollable delight, would approach Bahá'u'lláh and embrace Him. He would then embrace each of his fellow-prisoners and would go forth, with a heart filled with hope and joy, to meet the death that awaited him. Soon after the martyrdom of each of these heroic souls, the executioner, who had grown to admire Bahá'u'lláh, would come to Him and would inform Him of the circumstances of the death of the martyr and of the joy with which he had endured, to the very end, the pain inflicted upon him.

Exercises:

1.   What was the name of the prison in which Bahá'u'lláh was confined? _____
      _____

2.   What does "Síyáh-Chál" mean? _____

3.   For what was the Síyáh-Chál originally used? _____
      _____

4.   Describe the conditions of the Síyáh-Chál. _____
      _____
      _____
      _____
      _____
      _____
      _____
      _____
      _____
      _____
      _____
      _____
      _____
      _____

5.   Upon His arrival in the Síyáh-Chál, what was placed around the neck of Bahá'u'lláh?
      _____

6.   What were fastened around His feet?_____

7.   How were Bahá'u'lláh and His companions placed in their cell? _____
      _____

8.   What did Bahá'u'lláh teach them to do? _____

9. What would one row of the Bábís chant throughout the night? _____

_____

10. How would the other row respond? _____

_____

11. What effect did their chanting have on the King? _____

_____

12. Every day the jailors would come to the cell where Bahá'u'lláh and His companions were confined and call the name of one of the Bábís. In your own words, explain what would then happen. _____

_____

_____

_____

_____

_____

_____

_____

_____

_____

13. Why do you think the Bábís were so full of joy, despite the horrible conditions of their imprisonment? _____

_____

_____

SECTION 12

The terrible conditions under which Bahá'u'lláh and His companions were imprisoned in the Síyáh-Chál have been described by Bahá'u'lláh Himself. It will be important for you, then, to reflect on His own Words about the days spent in that dark dungeon. In one passage He says:

"Upon Our arrival We were first conducted along a pitch-black corridor, from whence We descended three steep flights of stairs to the place of confinement assigned to Us. The dungeon was wrapped in thick darkness, and Our fellow-prisoners numbered nearly hundred and fifty souls: thieves, assassins and highwaymen. Though crowded, it had no other outlet than the passage by which We entered. No pen can depict that place, nor any tongue describe its loathsome smell. Most of these men had neither clothes nor bedding to lie on. God alone knoweth what befell Us in that most foul-smelling and gloomy place!" [28]

Nabíl, the immortal historian of the Bahá'í Faith, recounts the words he himself heard from Bahá'u'lláh:

"All those who were struck down by the storm that raged during that memorable year in Ṭihrán were Our fellow-prisoners in the Síyáh-Chál, where We were confined. We were all huddled together in one cell, our feet in stocks, and around our necks fastened the most galling of chains. The air we breathed was laden with the foulest impurities, while the floor on which we sat was covered with filth and infested with vermin. No ray of light was allowed to penetrate that pestilential dungeon or to warm its icy-coldness. We were placed in two rows, each facing the other. We had taught them to repeat certain verses which, every night, they chanted with extreme fervor. 'God is sufficient unto me; He verily is the All-sufficing!' one row would intone, while the other would reply: 'In Him let the trusting trust.' The chorus of these gladsome voices would continue to peal out until the early hours of the morning. . . .

"Every day Our jailors, entering Our cell, would call the name of one of Our companions, bidding him arise and follow them to the foot of the gallows. With what eagerness would the owner of that name respond to that solemn call! Relieved of his chains, he would spring to his feet and, in a state of uncontrollable delight, would approach and embrace Us. We would seek to comfort him with the assurance of an everlasting life in the world beyond, and, filling his heart with hope and joy, would send him forth to win the crown of glory. He would embrace, in turn, the rest of his fellow-prisoners and then proceed to die as dauntlessly as he had lived. Soon after the martyrdom of each of these companions, We would be informed by the executioner, who had grown to be friendly to Us, of the circumstances of the death of his victim, and of the joy with which he had endured his sufferings to the very end." [29]

Exercises:

1. Complete the following sentences:

    a. Bahá'u'lláh tells us that, upon His arrival in the Síyáh-Chál, He was first conducted _____ .

    b. From the corridor, Bahá'u'lláh descended _____ _____ to the place of confinement assigned to Him.

    c. The dungeon was wrapped in _____ .

    d. In addition to Bahá'u'lláh and His companions, nearly hundred and fifty other souls were imprisoned in the Síyáh-Chál: _____, _____ and _____ .

    e. Though the dungeon was crowded, it had no other outlet than _____ _____ .

f. Bahá'u'lláh tells us that no pen can _____ and no tongue can _____ .

g. Most of the men had neither _____ nor _____ _____ .

2. Complete the following sentences:

a. Bahá'u'lláh tells us that all those who were struck down by _____ _____ during that year in Ṭihrán were His _____ _____ .

b. Bahá'u'lláh and His companions were huddled together in _____ , their feet in _____, and around their necks fastened _____ _____ .

c. The air they breathed was filled with _____ .

d. The floor on which they sat was covered with _____ and infested with _____ .

e. No ray of light was allowed to _____ _____ or to _____ .

f. Bahá'u'lláh and His companions were placed in two rows, _____ _____ .

g. Bahá'u'lláh taught them certain verses which, every night, they _____ _____ .

h. One row would intone the verse: " _____ _____ !"

i. And the other row would reply: " _____ _____ ."

j. The chorus of their voices would continue until _____ _____ .

k. Bahá'u'lláh tells us that every day their jailors would enter their cell and would call _____, bidding him to arise and _____

_____ .

l. With _____ the owner of that name would respond to that call.

m. Relieved of his chains, he would _____ and,

_____ , he would embrace Bahá'u'lláh.

n. Bahá'u'lláh would seek to comfort him with _____

_____ , and, filling his heart with hope and joy, would _____

_____ .

o. He would then embrace _____

and proceed to _____

_____ .

p. Soon after the martyrdom of each of these companions, Bahá'u'lláh would be informed by the executioner of the _____

_____ , and of the _____

_____ .

SECTION 13

There is a profound concept which every student of Bahá'í history must understand, namely, that the Cause of God advances through a series of crises and victories. The forces of ignorance, injustice, cruelty and fanaticism continually attack the Bahá'í community and give rise to crises. But each time, in accordance with the Will of God, the forces of darkness are defeated and the result is a victory. The Cause moves from crisis to victory to crisis to victory, and no power on earth is capable of stopping its onward march.

The short Ministry of the Báb had already followed such a course. The ordinary observer, however, would have assumed that the latest crisis could not be overcome: The Báb had been martyred. Thousands of His followers had been killed in a massacre of untold cruelty. The most outstanding of His disciples had been martyred, and the only One Who could revive hope was under chains in the darkest of dungeons. The crisis was indeed profound, but the victory that followed was most glorious.

In the Síyáh-Chál, God made known to Bahá'u'lláh the greatness of His Station. Wrapped in gloom, breathing the foulest of air, His feet in stocks, and His neck weighed down by a mighty chain, Bahá'u'lláh received the first intimations of God's Revelation. Under these dreadful circumstances, the "Most Great Spirit" revealed itself to Him, bidding Him to arise and speak forth the Word of God.

At times, He would feel as if something flowed from the crown of His head over His breast, as a mighty torrent falls upon the earth from the summit of a high mountain. He saw the Maiden of Heaven suspended before Him, speaking to His inner and outer being, referring to Him as the Best-Beloved of the worlds, the Beauty of God, and the power of God's sovereignty. He was assured that He would be made victorious by Himself and by His Pen, and by the aid of those whom God would raise up.

Thus, out of the darkness of the Black Pit rose the Sun of Truth. The Báb's promise had been fulfilled. The Bahá'í Revelation was born. Yet Bahá'u'lláh did not inform anyone of what had occurred. He would await the appointed hour, ordained by God, to make His Mission known.

Exercises:

1.   Describe in your own words how severe was the crisis in which the Bábí community found itself at the time of Bahá'u'lláh's imprisonment._____

_____

_____

_____

_____

_____

_____

_____

_____

_____

2.   What was the victory that followed? _____

_____

_____

_____

_____

_____

_____

_____

_____

SECTION 14

Humanity is fortunate to have this most momentous occurrence in religious history recorded in Bahá'u'lláh's own Words. Calling to mind the way God's Revelation first filled His soul, He says:

> **"One night, in a dream, these exalted words were heard on every side: 'Verily, We shall render Thee victorious by Thyself and by Thy Pen. Grieve Thou not for that which hath befallen Thee, neither be Thou afraid, for Thou art in safety. Erelong will God raise up the treasures of the earth—men who will aid Thee through Thyself and through Thy Name, wherewith God hath revived the hearts of such as have recognized Him.'"** [30]

In another passage He decribes the effect of God's Revelation on His being:

> **"During the days I lay in the prison of Ṭihrán, though the galling weight of the chains and the stench-filled air allowed Me but little sleep, still in those infrequent moments of slumber I felt as if something flowed from the crown of My head over My breast, even as a mighty torrent that precipitateth itself upon the earth from the summit of a lofty mountain. Every limb of My body would, as a result, be set afire. At such moments My tongue recited what no man could bear to hear."** [31]

Yet in another passage He describes how the Maiden, symbolizing the "Most Great Spirit", appeared to Him:

> **"While engulfed in tribulations I heard a most wondrous, a most sweet voice, calling above My head. Turning My face, I beheld a Maiden—the embodiment of the remembrance of the name of My Lord—suspended in the air before Me. So rejoiced was she in her very soul that her countenance shone with the ornament of the good-pleasure of God, and her cheeks glowed with the brightness of the All-Merciful. Betwixt earth and heaven she was raising a call which captivated the hearts and minds of men. She was imparting to both My inward and outer being tidings which rejoiced My soul, and the souls of God's honored servants. Pointing with her finger unto My head, she addressed all who are in heaven and all who are on earth, saying: 'By God! This is the Best-Beloved of the worlds, and yet ye comprehend not. This is the Beauty of God amongst you, and the power of His sovereignty within you, could ye but understand. This is the Mystery of God and His Treasure, the Cause of God and His glory unto all who are in the kingdoms of Revelation and of creation, if ye be of them that perceive.'"** [32]

Exercises:

1. Complete the following sentences:

   a. Bahá'u'lláh tells us that one night, in a dream, these words were heard on every side: "Verily, We shall render Thee _____ by

_____ and by _____. Grieve Thou not for that which hath _____, neither be Thou _____, for Thou art in _____. Erelong God will _____ the _____ of the earth—_____ who will aid Thee through _____ and through _____ _____, wherewith God hath _____ the hearts of such as have _____."

2.   Complete the following sentences:

   a.   During the days Bahá'u'lláh lay in _____ in Ṭihrán, the _____ of the _____ and the _____ allowed Him little _____ .

   b.   Though He slept little, still in those infrequent _____ _____ He felt as if _____ from _____ _____ over _____ .

   c.   As a result, every limb of His body _____ .

   d.   At such moments, Bahá'u'lláh recited what no man _____ _____ .

3.   Complete the following sentences:

   a.   Bahá'u'lláh says that while engulfed in tribulation, He heard _____ _____ , _____ , calling above His head.

   b.   Turning His face, Bahá'u'lláh beheld a Maiden suspended _____ _____ .

   c.   The face of the Maiden shone with _____ _____ and her cheeks glowed with _____ _____ .

   d.   The Maiden imparted to both His _____ tidings which rejoiced His _____ , and the souls of God's _____ _____ .

e. Pointing her finger to Bahá'u'lláh's head, she addressed these words to all who are in _____ and all who are on _____: "By God! This is the _____, and yet ye comprehend not. This is the _____ amongst you, and _____ within you, could ye but understand. This is the _____ and His _____, the _____ and His _____ unto all who are in the kingdoms of _____ and of _____, if ye be of them that perceive."

SECTION 15

So important is the concept of crisis and victory that it is worthwhile for you to pause at this point and reflect on the power of the Cause, which overcomes every obstacle in its path. To help you do so, it is suggested that you read the quotations below—one from the Writings of Bahá'u'lláh and the other from a letter written on behalf of Shoghi Effendi—and carry out the exercises that follow.

> "Behold how in this Dispensation the worthless and foolish have fondly imagined that by such instruments as massacre, plunder and banishment they can extinguish the Lamp which the Hand of Divine power hath lit, or eclipse the Day Star of everlasting splendor. How utterly unaware they seem to be of the truth that such adversity is the oil that feedeth the flame of this Lamp! Such is God's transforming power. He changeth whatsoever He willeth; He verily hath power over all things. . . ."[33]

> "This Cause, as every Divine Cause, cannot be effectively established unless it encounters and valiantly triumphs over the forces of opposition with which it is assailed. The history of the Faith is in itself a sufficient proof of that. Trials and persecutions have always been, and will continue to be, the lot of the chosen ones of God. But these they should consider as blessings in disguise, as through them their faith will be quickened, purified and strengthened. Bahá'u'lláh compares such afflictive trials to the oil which feeds the lamp of the Cause of God."[34]

Exercises:

1. Consult with one of the believers in your community who knows the history of the Faith well, and ask him or her to tell you about some of the crises and victories the Cause has experienced over the past few decades.

2. Consult with a member of your community who knows its history well, and ask him or her to tell you about what kind of opposition the Faith has experienced in your country and what the results have been.

3. How does knowing that the Faith advances through a series of crises and victories help you to react when calamities and difficulties occur in your own life? When trying to achieve goals you set for yourself, should you give up at the first sign of difficulty? _____

_____

_____

_____

_____

_____

_____

_____

SECTION 16

While Bahá'u'lláh remained under chains in the Síyáh-Chál, His enemies were busy trying to obtain His death sentence from the King. Bahá'u'lláh, however, was loved by people high and low alike and could not be executed so easily. Proof was needed that would connect Him with the attempt on the King's life. But the more they tried to find proof, the more it became evident that He was entirely innocent. Unable to prove guilt, these ruthless enemies decided to poison His food. So strong was the poison, however, that its initial effects were quickly noticed and Bahá'u'lláh stopped eating the poisonous meal they had offered Him. In the end, the authorities had no other choice but to release Him from prison, but this they did only on the condition that He would leave the country and go into exile.

Bahá'u'lláh had endured four months in prison. He was now ill and exhausted. The inhumane conditions of the prison, the chain of some 50 kilos around His neck, and finally the poison, had left Him in such a weakened state that He was confined to His bed under watchful care. The links of the chain had made deep wounds in His neck and, although these healed with time, the scars remained until the end of His life. In the midst of all this, the family had to prepare to undertake an arduous journey within one-month's time. Bahá'u'lláh had been given the freedom to choose the place of His exile. He chose Baghdád, then a city in the Ottoman Empire and today the capital of 'Iráq.

The trip lasted from 12 January 1853 to 8 April of the same year. It was the middle of winter, and Bahá'u'lláh and His family had to travel through the western part of Iran where winters are bitterly cold. The supplies they had for the journey were not sufficient, and they had to be content with little food. But the Protector of this small band of travelers was Almighty God Himself, and through His unfailing assistance, they arrived safely in Baghdád.

Iran had deprived itself of the bounty of the presence of Bahá'u'lláh and had forced Him to leave, never to return to His native land. 'Iráq was now to be the home of the most precious Being on the planet. An outstanding Bahá'í historian has these words to say about Bahá'u'lláh's exile from Iran:

"As Bahá'u'lláh neared the frontier, a period drew to its close. Were the people of Iran aware of the loss they sustained? Steeped in ignorance, sunk in bigotry, blinded by prejudice, led by self-seeking men, beguiled by falsehoods, theirs was not to see and know. And thus the Redeemer of the world passed out of their midst. He Who once was loved and respected by rich and poor, high and low, prince and peasant alike, was now deserted by the same people on whom He had lavished mercy, love, justice and charity at all times. Iran lost the presence of Bahá'u'lláh, but could His spirit ever be absent from that or any other land?" [35]

Exercises:

1. Why were Bahá'u'lláh's enemies unable to obtain His death sentence? _____

   _____

   _____

   _____

2. Bahá'u'lláh's enemies were unsuccessful in their schemes to connect Him with the attempt on the King's life. What did they then do? _____

   _____

   _____

3. How many months was Bahá'u'lláh in the Síyáh-Chál? _____

4. On what terms was He released? _____

   _____

5. What city did Bahá'u'lláh choose as the place of His exile? _____

6. Baghdád was then a city in _____, and today it is the capital of _____.

7. Bahá'u'lláh and His family began their journey to Baghdád on _____
   _____. It ended nearly three months later on _____.

8. Describe the conditions of the journey. _____

   _____

   _____

   _____

   _____

   _____

   _____

SECTION 17

The following prayer revealed by Bahá'u'lláh will help you get a glimpse of the suffering He experienced in the Síyáh-Chál and the hardships He endured in the months immediately after.

"My God, My Master, My Desire! . . . Thou hast created this atom of dust through the consummate power of Thy might, and nurtured Him with Thine hands which none can chain up. . . . The throat Thou didst accustom to the touch of silk Thou hast, in the end, clasped with strong chains, and the body Thou didst ease with brocades and velvets Thou hast at last subjected to the abasement of a dungeon. Thy decree hath shackled Me with unnumbered fetters, and cast about My neck chains that none can sunder. A number of years have passed during which afflictions have, like showers of mercy, rained upon Me. . . . How many the nights during which the weight of chains and fetters allowed Me no rest, and how numerous the days during which peace and tranquillity were denied Me, by reason of that wherewith the hands and tongues of men have afflicted Me! Both bread and water which Thou hast, through Thine all-embracing mercy, allowed unto the beasts of the field, they have, for a time, forbidden unto this servant, and the things they refused to inflict upon such as have seceded from Thy Cause, the same have they suffered to be inflicted upon Me, until, finally, Thy decree was irrevocably fixed, and Thy behest summoned this servant to depart out of Persia, accompanied by a number of frail-bodied men and children of tender age, at this time when the cold is so intense that one cannot even speak, and ice and snow so abundant that it is impossible to move." [36]

Exercise:

1. You may wish to memorize the above prayer. But even if you only read through it several times, a number of statements about Bahá'u'lláh's suffering will be impressed upon your mind. What are some of these?

SECTION 18

In Baghdád, Bahá'u'lláh rented a house in the old quarter of the city. In the months following His arrival, an increasing number of Bábís made their way to Baghdád. Unfortunately, many had sunk into a pitiful state; they were confused and bewildered, and some were committing acts unworthy of a follower of the Báb. Bahá'u'lláh received all those who arrived with boundless love and assisted them in cleansing their hearts and in reviving their spirits. Under His influence, the fortunes of the Bábí community began to change and hope blossomed again. But alas, a new crisis was in the making. This time its source was within the community itself; the cause of misfortune was none other than Bahá'u'lláh's own half-brother, Mírzá Yaḥyá, who claimed to be the Báb's successor.

In reality, the Báb had not seen the need to name a successor, for He knew that the Promise of All Ages would soon appear. What He had done was to nominate, on the advice of Bahá'u'lláh and another disciple, Mírzá Yaḥyá as a figure-head. This would enable Bahá'u'lláh to promote the Cause in relative security. Mírzá Yaḥyá had received much love and support from Bahá'u'lláh throughout his life, yet he was both ambitious and cowardly. The martyrdom of the Báb had shocked him to such an extent that he had almost lost his faith. He had wandered for a while as a dervish in the mountains of Mázindarán, his behavior so shameful that he had driven some of the Bábís of the region away from the Cause. Using one disguise after another, he had finally come to Baghdád, and having obtained a sum of money from Bahá'u'lláh in order to engage in commerce, was living under a new name in one of the neighborhoods of the city.

The growing respect and love being shown to Bahá'u'lláh by the followers of the Báb, as well as His rising prestige among the city officials, had a terrible effect on Mírzá Yaḥyá. His jealousy was aroused and its fire burned with such intensity that it consumed every trace of decency. Together with an associate more shameless than himself, Mírzá Yaḥyá set out to sow the seeds of doubt among the Bábís about Bahá'u'lláh's intentions. Once again the clouds of suspicion, fear and idle fancy descended upon the Bábí community. The short period of calm and tranquillity had come to an end and, day by day, Bahá'u'lláh's sufferings were intensifying.

On the morning of 10 April 1854, Bahá'u'lláh's family woke to find that He was gone. He had left the city without telling anyone His purpose or destination. Seeing where the actions of Mírzá Yaḥyá were leading, Bahá'u'lláh had chosen to retire to the mountains of Kurdistán, northeast of Baghdád. **"The one object of Our retirement"**, He Himself has later said, **"was to avoid becoming a subject of discord among the faithful, a source of disturbance unto Our companions, the means of injury to any soul, or the cause of sorrow to any heart."** [37]

In the wilderness, some distance from the town of Sulaymáníyyih, Bahá'u'lláh lived alone in communion with God. He was content with little food. At times He received some milk from the shepherds in the surrounding area and, occasionally, visited the town to obtain the minimum necessities of life. Yet, even during these brief contacts with the people of the region, Bahá'u'lláh's greatness could not be kept hidden from their eyes. His love and wisdom attracted the inhabitants of Sulaymáníyyih and His fame began to spread to the neighboring areas. News of a man of extraordinary wisdom and eloquence living in that region of Kurdistán finally reached Baghdád. His family, realizing that this Personage could be none other than Bahá'u'lláh, sent a trusted believer to beg Him to return. Bahá'u'lláh accepted their request, thus ending His two-year voluntary withdrawal.

Exercises:

1. In what state were the Bábís who made their way to Baghdád following Bahá'u'lláh's arrival in that city? _____

   _____

2. Why had they fallen into such a state?_____

   _____

   _____

3. What began to happen to the Bábí community under the influence of Bahá'u'lláh?

   _____

   _____

   _____

4. Had the Báb named a successor? Why not? _____

   _____

   _____

5. Whom had the Báb named as a figure-head? _____

6. What was Mírzá Yaḥyá's relationship to Bahá'u'lláh? _____

7. Describe Mírzá Yaḥyá's character. _____

   _____

   _____

8. What had Mírzá Yaḥyá done after the martyrdom of the Báb? _____

   _____

   _____

   _____

   _____

   _____

   _____

   _____

   _____

9. What effect did Bahá'u'lláh's growing influence on the Bábí community have on Mírzá Yaḥyá? _____

_____

10. What did Bahá'u'lláh do when He saw where Mírzá Yaḥyá's actions were leading?

_____

_____

11. To what region did Bahá'u'lláh retire? _____

12. Bahá'u'lláh tells us that the one object of His retirement was to avoid becoming a subject of _____, a source of __ _____, the means of _____, or the cause of _____ _____ .

13. What did Bahá'u'lláh do in the wilderness of Kurdistán? _____

_____

_____

_____

14. How long did Bahá'u'lláh's withdrawal from Baghdád last? _____

15. What were the circumstances that led to His return? _____

_____

_____

SECTION 19

Every Manifestation of God makes a Covenant with His followers. The followers of the Báb had entered into a Covenant with Him to seek and accept Him Whom God would make manifest and to live in obedience to His commands. Although Bahá'u'lláh had not yet told others that He was the One promised by the Báb, His greatness was becoming more and more apparent with each passing day, and a few had even begun to recognize His Station. Mírzá Yaḥyá was not blind to Bahá'u'lláh's majesty and glory. But his jealousy and ambition were aroused, causing him to engage in mischief which would finally lead him to openly break the Covenant of the Báb. Referring to the turmoil and tribulations which were awaiting them, Bahá'u'lláh warned the friends:

"The days of tests are now come. Oceans of dissension and tribulation are surging, and the Banners of Doubt are, in every nook and corner, occupied in

stirring up mischief and in leading men to perdition. . . . Suffer not the voice of some of the soldiers of negation to cast doubt into your midst, neither allow yourselves to become heedless of Him Who is the Truth, inasmuch as in every Dispensation such contentions have been raised. God, however, will establish His Faith, and manifest His light albeit the stirrers of sedition abhor it. . . . Watch ye every day for the Cause of God. . . . All are held captive in His grasp. No place is there for any one to flee to. Think not the Cause of God to be a thing lightly taken, in which any one can gratify his whims. In various quarters a number of souls have, at the present time, advanced this same claim. The time is approaching when . . . every one of them will have perished and been lost, nay will have come to naught and become a thing unremembered, even as the dust itself." [38]

Exercises:

1.　What does the word "turmoil" mean? _____

_____

2.　Complete the following sentences:

a.　Bahá'u'lláh told the friends not to allow the _____ of some of the

_____ to cast _____

_____.

b.　He warned them not to allow themselves to become _____ of

_____.

c.　He assured the friends that God would establish _____ and

manifest _____ even if the enemies of the Cause reject it.

d.　The friends should not think that the Cause of God is a _____

_____, in which any one can _____ his

_____.

e.　The time will come when all those who have turned against the Faith will have

_____ and been _____. Like the dust, they

will all become a thing _____.

3.　Who are "the soldiers of negation"? _____

_____

4.　Are there soldiers of negation in the world today? _____

5.   What should we do if we encounter them? _____

_____

_____

_____

_____

SECTION 20

During Bahá'u'lláh's absence, the fortunes of the Faith had reached the lowest point in its history. As expected, Mírzá Yaḥyá had proved himself to be incapable of leading even the small community in Baghdád. In various parts, a number of the Bábís were engaged in activities that brought shame to the precious Cause of the Báb. So, once again, Bahá'u'lláh took on the task of reviving the community. His arrival in March 1856 was announced to the believers, and His door was opened to all who longed for truth. The modest residence in which He lived with His family became the center wherein gathered seekers, visitors and pilgrims. Everyone who came into His presence was transformed by the power of His sweet and loving words. Those who had the bounty of living in close proximity to Him felt as if they were in paradise. They became a new creation, utterly detached from the things of this world. This is how Nabíl, the great historian of the early Bahá'í Era, has described the state of those souls:

> "Many a night, no less than ten persons subsisted on no more than a pennyworth of dates. No one knew to whom actually belonged the shoes, the cloaks, or the robes that were to be found in their houses. Whoever went to the bazaar could claim that the shoes upon their feet were his own, and each one who entered the presence of Bahá'u'lláh could affirm that the cloak and robe he then wore belonged to him. Their own names they had forgotten, their hearts were emptied of aught else except adoration for their Beloved. . . . O, for the joy of those days, and the gladness and wonder of those hours!" [39]

Bahá'u'lláh remained in Baghdád for seven years following His return from Sulaymáníyyih. During this time, He continued to keep hidden His Station as the Manifestation of God for this Day. Yet Divine love poured out from Him in such measure that receptive hearts could not but be touched by it. The Divine guidance He revealed in conversations and in written verses and tablets transformed the character of the Bábís who had been left shepherdless for so many years. These are the years during which He revealed the Book of Certitude, wherein He explained the nature of God's Revelation in such clear terms that the foundations of man-made dogmas of the past were destroyed. It is during this same period that He revealed, as He walked the banks of river Tigris wrapped in meditation, the Hidden Words, so cherished by every one of us as a guide to our spiritual growth. The rapidity with which revealed verses flowed from His Pen was astonishing. This is how He Himself has referred to that period of extraordinary potency:

> ". . . We revealed, as a copious rain, by the aid of God and His Divine Grace and mercy, Our verses, and sent them to various parts of the world. We exhorted all men, and particularly this people, through Our wise counsels and

loving admonitions, and forbade them to engage in sedition, quarrels, disputes and conflict. As a result of this, and by the grace of God, waywardness and folly were changed into piety and understanding, and weapons converted into instruments of peace." [40]

The seven years of Bahá'u'lláh's life in Baghdád represent a period of magnificent victories. It was to be expected, then, that sooner or later a crisis should arise, which in turn would be followed by an even greater victory. The growing prestige of Bahá'u'lláh did not go unnoticed by the enemies of the Faith. The most active among them was a certain Shaykh who used every means at his disposal to convince the officials of both the Persian and Ottoman Governments, as well as the clergy, to rise in opposition against Him. But for years the Shaykh's efforts were frustrated by Bahá'u'lláh's wisdom and the nobility of His words and deeds.

One time, for example, this Shaykh called together the most distinguished clergy in the region with the intention of obtaining their unanimous condemnation of Bahá'u'lláh. All were prepared to launch an attack against the small band of exiles in Baghdád in order to destroy the Faith at its heart. To their surprise, however, the most highly placed among them, a man known for his justice and piety, refused to give the necessary sentence against the Bábís. He told the group that, to his knowledge, the Bábí community had done nothing that would justify such an act and left the gathering.

Since its original plan failed, the group decided to send a learned man to Bahá'u'lláh and to submit to Him a number of questions in order to test His knowledge. When Bahá'u'lláh replied to all the questions, this messenger accepted, on behalf of the group of clergy, the vastness of His knowledge. But then, he said, in order to satisfy everyone concerned of the truth of His Mission, He should perform a miracle for them. "Although you have no right to ask this," Bahá'u'lláh replied, "for God should test His creatures, and they should not test God, still I allow and accept this request." [41] He told the messenger, however, that first the clergy should choose one miracle and write down that, after its performance, they would no longer have any doubts about Him and they would all recognize Him and would confess the truth of His Cause. They should seal this document and bring it to Him.

This clear and challenging reply affected the messenger profoundly. He instantly arose, kissed the knee of Bahá'u'lláh, and departed. He delivered Bahá'u'lláh's message to the group of clergy. They debated over it for three days, but could not come to any decision. Finally, they had no other choice but to drop the matter.

But these ruthless enemies of the Faith did not give up their schemings against Bahá'u'lláh. They continued to stir up mischief and to misrepresent His intentions to the authorities, until at last, in the spring of 1863, their efforts yielded fruit, and the next crisis appeared.

Exercises:

1.   In what condition was the Bábí community when Bahá'u'lláh returned to Baghdád?

   _____

   _____

2.   Had Mírzá Yaḥyá proved himself capable of leading the community? _____

3.   What effect did Bahá'u'lláh's return to Baghdád have on the Bábís? _____

     _____

     _____

     _____

     _____

4.   Express in your own words Nabil's description of the state of those who lived close to Bahá'u'lláh. _____

     _____

     _____

     _____

     _____

     _____

     _____

     _____

     _____

     _____

5.   How many years did Bahá'u'lláh remain in Baghdád following His return from Sulaymáníyyih? _____

6.   Mention two of the Works revealed by Bahá'u'lláh during those seven years in Baghdád. _____

7.   What is the main theme of the Book of Certitude? _____

     _____

8.   What does the phrase "man-made dogmas" mean? Can you mention one or two examples? _____

     _____

     _____

     _____

     _____

9.   What kind of subjects do the Hidden Words address? _____

     _____

     _____

10. Complete the following sentences:

    a. Bahá'u'lláh tells us that by the _____ of God and His_____ _____ and _____, He revealed His verses as _____.

    b. He sent these verses to _____.

    c. In these verses, He _____ all men through His _____ _____ and _____.

    d. He forbade them to _____ in _____, _____, _____, and _____.

    e. As a result of this, and by the grace of God, _____ and _____ were changed into _____ and _____ , and _____ were converted into _____ of _____.

11. How did Bahá'u'lláh's growing prestige affect the enemies of the Faith?_____
_____
_____

12. What does the phrase "unanimous condemnation" mean? _____
_____
_____

13. Relate in your own words the story of the group of clergy and the messenger they sent to Bahá'u'lláh in Baghdád. _____
_____
_____
_____
_____
_____
_____
_____
_____
_____
_____
_____

14.   Why did the group decide not to pursue its request that Bahá'u'lláh perform a miracle? _____

_____

_____

_____

SECTION 21

In the course of your studies of the Faith, you will read the Book of Certitude and will reflect on the profound meaning of its many themes. You are, of course, already familiar with the Hidden Words. This volume will be a constant companion to you throughout your life, and the divine guidance contained therein will have great influence on your spiritual development. At this point, while you are reflecting on the period of Bahá'u'lláh's life in Baghdád, during which these two important Books were revealed, you may wish to memorize the opening passage of each. The Book of Certitude opens thus:

> **"No man shall attain the shores of the ocean of true understanding except he be detached from all that is in heaven and on earth. Sanctify your souls, O ye peoples of the world, that haply ye may attain that station which God hath destined for you and enter thus the tabernacle which, according to the dispensations of Providence, hath been raised in the firmament of the Bayán."** [42]

And the opening passage of the Hidden Words reads:

> **"This is that which hath descended from the realm of glory, uttered by the tongue of power and might, and revealed unto the Prophets of old. We have taken the inner essence thereof and clothed it in the garment of brevity, as a token of grace unto the righteous, that they may stand faithful unto the Covenant of God, may fulfill in their lives His trust, and in the realm of spirit obtain the gem of divine virtue."** [43]

SECTION 22

Towards the end of His stay in Baghdád, Bahá'u'lláh began to make occasional reference to the tests and trials that lay ahead. A dream He once related to the friends caused them great distress. **"I saw,"** He wrote in a Tablet, **"the Prophets and the Messengers gather and seat themselves around Me, moaning, weeping and loudly lamenting. Amazed, I inquired of them the reason, whereupon their lamentation and weeping** waxed greater, and they said unto Me: 'We weep for Thee, O Most Great Mystery, O Tabernacle of Immortality!' They wept with such a weeping that I too wept with them. Thereupon the Concourse on high addressed Me saying: '. . . Erelong shalt Thou behold with Thine own eyes what no Prophet hath beheld. . . . Be patient, be patient.' . . . They continued addressing Me the whole night until the approach of dawn." [44]

Early in 1863, during the twelve-day festival of Naw-Rúz marking the Persian new year, Bahá'u'lláh revealed the Tablet of the Holy Mariner which, in a mystical language, foretold future events and spoke of betrayal and separation. This Tablet was read to the friends gathered in His presence on 26 March. Oceans of sorrow surged in their hearts as they sensed that He was to be taken from them. That very day, a messenger delivered to Bahá'u'lláh a communication requesting an interview between Him and the Governor of Baghdád. On the following day, Bahá'u'lláh was presented with a letter from the Prime Minister of the Ottoman Empire to the Governor, worded in a courteous manner, inviting Bahá'u'lláh to travel to the Ottoman capital, Constantinople. A mounted escort was ordered to accompany Him for His protection. Bahá'u'lláh agreed to the request at once, but refused to accept the money that the government was offering for His travels. The Governor's representative insisted He accept it, saying that the authorities would be offended if He did not do so. Finally, He took the generous sum and immediately distributed it among the poor of the city.

News of Bahá'u'lláh's exile from Baghdád shook the Bábí community. The friends were overwhelmed with sadness, and, at first, no one was able to sleep or eat. Gradually, however, they were calmed through Bahá'u'lláh's kind and tender words and accepted that most would be deprived of the bounty of accompanying Him on the next stage of His exile. As token of His love, He wrote in His own handwriting a Tablet for each of the friends who lived in the city—man, woman, and child.

In the vicinity of Baghdád, there was a beautiful garden full of roses, and the rose was Bahá'u'lláh's favorite flower. Thirty-one days after Naw-Rúz, He left the city and entered the garden. The believers, and indeed vast numbers of the people of Baghdád, were grief stricken. The Bábí community, now totally revived through the tender care of Bahá'u'lláh, had entered yet another crisis. What would be the future of this young Faith whose only Hope was being exiled to a place so far away from the majority of its adherents? The answer awaiting those heartbroken Bábís who gathered to bid Him farewell was stupendous. Bahá'u'lláh would tear away the veils that hid His true Station from the eyes of men and would openly declare that He was the Promised One of all ages.

Bahá'u'lláh stayed in the garden, known today as the Garden of Riḍván, for twelve days before departing for Constantinople. His enemies had tried to strike a fatal blow at His Cause by separating Him from the majority of the believers. God, however, turned the farewell into an occasion of immense joy. The declaration of His Mission created new life in the souls of His companions. This was the Day of Days for which the Báb had prepared them. Bahá'u'lláh Himself has said that on that Day **"all created things were immersed in the sea of purification"**. [45]

Unfortunately there is little known of the details of the conversations Bahá'u'lláh held with the stream of visitors He received in the Garden of Riḍván. The following words of the historian Nabíl give us only a glimpse of the glory of those days:

"Every day, ere the hour of dawn, the gardeners would pick the roses which lined the four avenues of the garden, and would pile them in the center of the floor of His blessed tent. So great would be the heap that when His companions gathered to drink their morning tea in His presence, they would be unable to see each other across it. All these roses Bahá'u'lláh would, with His own hands, entrust to those whom He dismissed from His presence every morning to be delivered, on His behalf, to His Arab and Persian friends in the city. . . . One night, the ninth night of the waxing moon, I happened to be one of those who watched beside His blessed tent. As the hour of midnight approached, I saw Him issue from His tent, pass by the places where some of His companions were sleeping, and begin to pace up and down the moonlit, flower-bordered avenues of the garden. So loud was the singing of the nightingales on every side that only those who were near Him could hear distinctly His voice. He continued to walk until, pausing in the midst of one of these avenues, He observed: 'Consider these nightingales. So great is their love for these roses, that sleepless from dusk till dawn, they warble their melodies and commune with burning passion with the object of their adoration. How then can those who claim to be afire with the rose-like beauty of the Beloved choose to sleep?' For three successive nights I watched and circled round His blessed tent. Every time I passed by the couch whereon He lay, I would find Him wakeful, and every day, from morn till eventide, I would see Him ceaselessly engaged in conversing with the stream of visitors who kept flowing in from Baghdád. Not once could I discover in the words He spoke any trace of dissimulation." [46]

Today, the Bahá'ís of the world celebrate the twelve days from 21 April to 2 May as the Festival of Riḍván, the holiest and most significant of all Bahá'í festivals.

Exercises:

1. Recount in your own words the dream Bahá'u'lláh had towards the end of His stay in Baghdád. _____

    _____

    _____

    _____

    _____

    _____

2. What was the significance of the dream? _____

    _____

    _____

3. When did Bahá'u'lláh reveal the Tablet of the Holy Mariner? _____

    _____

4. What did the Tablet of the Holy Mariner foretell?_____

    _____

5. What did the messenger from the government bring to Bahá'u'lláh on the day the Tablet was read to the friends? _____

_____

6. What was presented to Bahá'u'lláh the following day? _____

_____

_____

7. Where had the government decided to send Bahá'u'lláh? _____

_____

8. Why had the government decided to send Him away from Baghdád? _____

_____

_____

9. What did Bahá'u'lláh do with the sum of money the government had offered Him for His travels? _____

_____

10. How did the friends react to the news of Bahá'u'lláh's approaching departure?

_____

_____

_____

11. What did Bahá'u'lláh do as a sign of His love for the friends? _____

_____

_____

12. By what name is the garden where Bahá'u'lláh declared His Mission now known?

_____

13. How many days did He remain in this garden? _____

14. Referring to those glorious days Bahá'u'lláh spent in the Garden of Riḍván, Nabíl tells us:

    a. Every day at the hour of dawn, the gardeners would _____

    _____, and would

    _____

    _____ .

b. So great would be the heap of roses that when Bahá'u'lláh's companions

_____ in His

presence, they would _____

_____.

c. All these roses Bahá'u'lláh would, with His own hands, entrust to those whom He dismissed from His presence every morning to be delivered, on His behalf,

_____.

d. One night, Nabíl happened to be one of those who _____

_____.

e. As the hour of midnight approached, Nabíl saw Bahá'u'lláh issue _____

_____, pass by _____

_____, and

begin _____

_____.

f. So loud was _____

_____ that only those who were near Bahá'u'lláh could

_____.

g. Bahá'u'lláh continued to walk until, _____

_____, He observed: "Consider these

_____. So great is their _____ for these

_____, that _____ from _____ till

_____, they _____ their _____ and

_____ with _____ with the

_____ of their _____. How then can

those who _____ to be _____ with the _____

_____ of the _____ choose to _____?"

h. For three successive nights Nabíl _____

_____.

i. Every time Nabíl passed by the couch on which Bahá'u'lláh lay, he would

_____, and every day, from morning till evening,

he would _____

_____

_____.

    j.   Not once could Nabíl discover in the words Bahá'u'lláh spoke _____

_____ .

15.   What had the enemies of the Faith tried to accomplish by separating Bahá'u'lláh from the majority of the believers, and what had God willed instead? _____

_____

_____

_____

_____

16.   What festival do we celebrate today as the anniversary of the Declaration of Bahá'u'lláh's Mission? _____

17.   How long does the Festival of Riḍván last, and on what dates is it celebrated?

_____

18.   Now that you have completed the study of Bahá'u'lláh's banishment from Iran to 'Iráq, prepare and deliver a short talk on this period of His life.

SECTION 23

Below are passages from a Tablet revealed by Bahá'u'lláh. Read them aloud with fervor. As you do so, call to mind Bahá'u'lláh's Declaration in the Garden of Riḍván and let His Words fill your heart with joy.

"The Divine Springtime is come, O Most Exalted Pen, for the Festival of the All-Merciful is fast approaching. Bestir thyself, and magnify, before the entire creation, the name of God, and celebrate His praise, in such wise that all created things may be regenerated and made new. Speak, and hold not thy peace. The day star of blissfulness shineth above the horizon of Our name, the Blissful, inasmuch as the kingdom of the name of God hath been adorned with the ornament of the name of thy Lord, the Creator of the heavens. Arise before the nations of the earth, and arm thyself with the power of this Most Great Name, and be not of those who tarry. . . .

"Canst thou discover any one but Me, O Pen, in this Day? What hath become of the creation and the manifestations thereof? What of the names and their kingdom? Whither are gone all created things, whether seen or unseen? What of the hidden secrets of the universe and its revelations? Lo, the entire creation hath passed away! Nothing remaineth except My Face, the Ever-Abiding, the Resplendent, the All-Glorious.

"This is the Day whereon naught can be seen except the splendors of the Light that shineth from the face of Thy Lord, the Gracious, the Most Bountiful. Verily, We have caused every soul to expire by virtue of Our irresistible and

all-subduing sovereignty. We have, then, called into being a new creation, as a token of Our grace unto men. I am, verily, the All-Bountiful, the Ancient of Days. . . .

"Say: This is the Paradise on whose foliage the wine of utterance hath imprinted the testimony: 'He that was hidden from the eyes of men is revealed, girded with sovereignty and power!' This is the Paradise, the rustling of whose leaves proclaims: 'O ye that inhabit the heavens and the earth! There hath appeared what hath never previously appeared. He Who, from everlasting, had concealed His Face from the sight of creation is now come.' From the whispering breeze that wafteth amidst its branches there cometh the cry: 'He Who is the sovereign Lord of all is made manifest. The Kingdom is God's,' while from its streaming waters can be heard the murmur: 'All eyes are gladdened, for He Whom none hath beheld, Whose secret no one hath discovered, hath lifted the veil of glory, and uncovered the countenance of Beauty.'

"Within this Paradise, and from the heights of its loftiest chambers, the Maids of Heaven have cried out and shouted: 'Rejoice, ye dwellers of the realms above, for the fingers of Him Who is the Ancient of Days are ringing, in the name of the All-Glorious, the Most Great Bell, in the midmost heart of the heavens. The hands of bounty have borne round the cup of everlasting life. Approach, and quaff your fill. Drink with healthy relish, O ye that are the very incarnations of longing, ye who are the embodiments of vehement desire!'" [47]

SECTION 24

Bahá'u'lláh, His family, and the small group of believers accompanying them stayed in Constantinople for only four months. The Persian Government continued from afar its persecution of the One it now clearly saw as the leader of the Bábí movement. Its Ambassador in the court of the Sulṭán, the ruler of the Ottoman Empire, mounted a systematic campaign against Bahá'u'lláh. The environment in which the Sulṭán, his ministers and their associates lived was one of treachery, intrigue, and hypocrisy. Bahá'u'lláh refused to have anything to do with these unworthy people. His aloofness made it even easier for the Persian Ambassador to fill the minds of the authorities with accusations and lies. His ceaseless efforts were effective and finally an order was issued exiling Bahá'u'lláh to the city of Adrianople, still farther from the Persian border.

Bahá'u'lláh's response to the order was an act of extraordinary courage. He immediately revealed a lengthy Tablet in which He addressed the Sulṭán himself, rebuked him and his ministers, and exposed their immaturity and incompetence. The Tablet was delivered to the Prime Minister in a sealed envelope. It is said that when he opened the letter and began to read it, he turned pale and remarked: "It is as if the King of Kings were issuing his behest to his humblest vassal king and regulating his conduct." [48]

The twelve-day journey from Constantinople to Adrianople was extremely difficult for Bahá'u'lláh and His family, who had now set out on their third exile. It was the month of December and the weather was extremely cold. Most of the exiles did not have the necessary clothes to protect them from such harsh weather. Even to obtain water from springs on their way, they had to light a fire to thaw the ice.

Bahá'u'lláh entered Adrianople on 12 December 1863 and stayed in that city for a total of four and a half years. This period again was one of painful crises and splendid victories. As the influence of Bahá'u'lláh grew, the fire of jealousy burned more fiercely in Mírzá Yaḥyá's heart. He became bolder and bolder in his opposition and tried his best to prevent the Bábís from accepting the Manifestation of God for this Day. The trouble he caused not only affected the community itself, but also gave the external enemies of the Faith ammunition which they used to launch further attacks against Bahá'u'lláh and His followers. Mírzá Yaḥyá's treachery seemed to have no bounds. He even decided to poison Bahá'u'lláh, and schemed and worked until he finally achieved his purpose. The effect of the poison on Bahá'u'lláh was grave, and although He recovered, He was left with a shaking hand until the end of His life.

Adrianople, of course, will not be remembered for the shameful acts of Mírzá Yaḥyá, but for the great victories that Bahá'u'lláh achieved in that city. It was from here that Bahá'u'lláh sent many of His Tablets addressed to the kings and rulers of the world and proclaimed His Faith far and wide.

This public proclamation was the third stage of a gradual process through which Bahá'u'lláh's Mission was made known to humanity. The first stage began in the dungeon of Síyáh-Chál in Ṭihrán when the Divine Spirit revealed itself to Bahá'u'lláh and announced to Him that He was the Bearer of God's Message for today. Although the birth of His Revelation remained unknown for a decade, like the dawn, it stirred sleeping souls, gradually awakening the receptive ones and preparing them to recognize Bahá'u'lláh. The second stage opened in the Garden of Riḍván, where He declared His Mission to certain of the believers gathered to bid Him farewell. Now a small number of favored souls were aware of His Station. The third stage was the universal proclamation of His Mission. It began in Constantinople, gained considerable momentum in Adrianople, and reached its greatest heights of power in 'Akká, the next and final place of His exile.

Exercises:

1.   How long did Bahá'u'lláh remain in Constantinople?_____

2.   Why was His stay there so brief? _____
     _____

3.   What does the word "aloofness" mean?_____
     _____

4.   Why did Bahá'u'lláh not become involved with the Sulṭán's court?_____
     _____
     _____

5.   To where was He next banished? _____

6.   Why did the Persian Government want Him sent farther away from its borders?

     _____

     _____

7.   What did Bahá'u'lláh do upon receiving news of His banishment? _____

     _____

     _____

8.   What did the Prime Minister remark when he read Bahá'u'lláh's letter? _____

     _____

     _____

     _____

9.   When did Bahá'u'lláh arrive in Adrianople? _____

10. How long did He remain in that city? _____

11. What was the most significant development that took place in Adrianople? _____

     _____

12. Through how many stages did the declaration of Bahá'u'lláh's Mission to humanity
     pass? _____

13. What was the first stage? ___SÍYÁH-CHÁL_____

     _____

14. What was the second stage? ___RIḌVÁN_____

     _____

15. What was the third stage? ___UNIVERSAL PROCLAMATION TO THE WORLD___

     _____

SECTION 25

     Mírzá Yaḥyá's open opposition to Bahá'u'lláh in Adrianople caused great turmoil
among the believers, many of whom were just beginning to get a glimpse of Bahá'u'lláh's
Station. This gave the enemies of the Cause, who had behind them the powers of two
governments—the Persian and the Ottoman—the opportunity they needed to strike another
blow at the newly born Faith of God. Suddenly one morning, the house of Bahá'u'lláh

was surrounded by soldiers, and everyone was told to prepare for immediate departure. For some time, no one knew what their destiny would be. The greatest fear of most was to be separated from their Beloved, for there were rumors that Bahá'u'lláh and His family would be exiled to one place and that the others would be forced to disperse. Finally it became clear that Bahá'u'lláh was to be banished to the prison-city of 'Akká and Mírzá Yaḥyá to the island of Cyprus. Most of the exiles, numbering about seventy, were sent to 'Akká including the two most vicious supporters of Mírzá Yaḥyá. Four of the companions of Bahá'u'lláh, on the other hand, were exiled with Mírzá Yaḥyá's group to Cyprus.

Bahá'u'lláh and His family left Adrianople on 12 August 1868, and after a difficult journey by land and sea, arrived in 'Akká on 31 August. The inhabitants of 'Akká were accustomed to the arrival of prisoners, for the city was used by the Ottomans as a place of banishment for criminals and agitators. This time, they were told that the new arrivals were enemies of the State, of God and His religion. The Sulṭán had ordered to keep them in strict confinement, and he and his ministers had expressed the hope that the harsh conditions of 'Akká would lead to their eventual extermination. The order of the Sulṭán had been read publicly in the mosque, and it was understood by all that these Persians had been condemned to perpetual imprisonment and that association with them was strictly forbidden.

After disembarking at 'Akká, the exiles were taken to the army barracks, a section of which was to be their prison. The first night, they were deprived of food and drink, and afterwards they were each assigned three loaves of low quality bread a day. Soon everyone, except for two, fell sick and, shortly after, three of them died. The guards refused to bury the dead without being paid the necessary expenses. A small prayer rug used by Bahá'u'lláh was sold, and the sum was given to the guards. Later, it was learned that they had not kept their word and had buried the dead unwashed, unshrouded and without coffins. They had in fact been given twice the amount required for the burial.

Although the conditions of imprisonment gradually improved, the first years in 'Akká were a period of severe suffering for Bahá'u'lláh. What He had endured in the Síyáh-Chál had been inflicted upon Him solely by the external enemies of the Faith. The turmoil in Adrianople was internal in character. The crisis of those first years in 'Akká, however, was the result of the workings of both the external and internal enemies of the Faith. He Himself has referred to this period in words such as the following:

"Know thou that upon Our arrival at this Spot, We chose to designate it as the 'Most Great Prison'. Though previously subjected in another land to chains and fetters, We yet refused to call it by that name. Say: Ponder thereon, O ye endued with understanding!" [49]

In spite of the order of the Sulṭán that no one should associate with Bahá'u'lláh and His family, a number of believers in Persia made the long journey to 'Akká, often on foot, with the hope that they might be admitted into His presence. Upon arrival, these devoted souls, unable to approach Him, would stand at a distance facing His prison, content to catch even a glimpse of His figure through the bars of His window. A wave of His blessed Hand was sufficient reward for months of travel, and most would then turn homeward, thankful for the bounty they had received.

The most tragic event of this period was the sudden death of Bahá'u'lláh's son Mírzá Mihdí, known as the Purest Branch. One evening, he was on the roof of the barracks, pacing back and forth in prayer and meditation, when he fell through a skylight onto a wooden crate on the floor below. His ribs were pierced, and, though a doctor was called in, there was nothing to be done. Within twenty-two hours, he was dead. Before his passing, Bahá'u'lláh asked the Purest Branch what he wished. He replied: "I wish the people of Bahá to be able to attain Your presence." "And so it shall be," Bahá'u'lláh said; "God will grant your wish." [50]

Severe as Bahá'u'lláh's sufferings were in the Most Great Prison, it must be remembered that His banishment to 'Akká was the fulfillment of the prophecies of the past. It was in 'Akká that the Sun of Truth would shine for twenty-four years in its full splendor. It would be during this period that while visiting Mount Carmel in nearby Haifa, Bahá'u'lláh would point out to 'Abdu'l-Bahá the place where the Shrine of the Báb would later be built. It would be His own resting place situated in the vicinity of 'Akká that would constitute the Holiest Spot on earth and the Qiblih of the people of Bahá. It would be in the vicinity of the Holy Shrine of the Báb that the Seat of the Universal House of Justice would be established. The twin cities of Haifa and 'Akká would become the spiritual and administrative world center of the Bahá'í Faith. He had already alluded in a Tablet to His banishment to 'Akká saying that: **"Upon Our arrival We were welcomed with banners of light, whereupon the Voice of the Spirit cried out saying: 'Soon will all that dwell on earth be enlisted under these banners.'"** [51]

Exercises:

1.   How did the enemies of the Faith use the trouble caused by Mírzá Yaḥyá to their advantage? _____

_____

2.   To where was Bahá'u'lláh next banished?_____

3.   Where was Mírzá Yaḥyá sent? _____

4.   How many accompanied Bahá'u'lláh to 'Akká? _____

5.   Why do you think some of Bahá'u'lláh's followers were sent to Cyprus with Mírzá Yaḥyá and two of Yaḥyá's supporters sent to 'Akká? _____

_____

_____

6.   On what date did Bahá'u'lláh depart from Adrianople? _____

7.   On what date did He arrive in 'Akká? _____

8.   What orders had the Sulṭán given regarding the imprisonment of Bahá'u'lláh and the believers accompanying Him? _____

_____

_____

9.   How did the people of 'Akká learn about the orders? _____
_____

10.   Where were Bahá'u'lláh and His companions taken upon their arrival in 'Akká?
_____

11.   In your own words describe the conditions of their first few days in the prison.

_____
_____
_____
_____
_____

12.   By what name did Bahá'u'lláh designate 'Akká? _____

13.   What was the most tragic event to occur during the early years in 'Akká? _____
_____

14.   In your own words, describe the circumstances surrounding the death of the Purest
Branch. _____
_____
_____
_____
_____
_____
_____
_____

15.   How many years did Bahá'u'lláh stay in 'Akká and its vicinity? _____

16.   What does the word "qiblih" mean? _____

17.   What is the Qiblih of the people of Bahá, and where is it located? _____
_____

18.   What did Bahá'u'lláh point out to 'Abdu'l-Bahá while visiting Mount Carmel in
Haifa? _____

19.   Where is the Seat of the Universal House of Justice located? _____
_____

20.   Where is the spiritual and administrative world center of the Bahá'í Faith? _____

_____

21.   Under what circumstances did the first pilgrims make their way to 'Akká? _____

_____

_____

_____

_____

_____

_____

22.   Do you know what pilgrims do today when they visit Haifa and 'Akká? You may
        wish to ask one of the friends in your community who has been to the Holy Land
        on pilgrimage to tell you about it.

SECTION 26

In 'Akká Bahá'u'lláh continued His universal proclamation. Here are some passages He addressed from Adrianople and 'Akká to the kings and rulers of the world:

To the Emperor of the French, Napoleon III:

> **"O King of Paris! Tell the priest to ring the bells no longer. By God, the True
> One! The Most Mighty Bell hath appeared in the form of Him Who is the
> Most Great Name . . ."** [52]

To Nicolaevitch Alexander II, the Czar of Russia:

> **"Arise thou amongst men in the name of this all-compelling Cause, and sum-
> mon, then, the nations unto God, the Exalted, the Great."** [53]

To Queen Victoria of England:

> **"Lay aside thy desire, and set then thine heart towards thy Lord, the Ancient
> of Days. We make mention of thee for the sake of God, and desire that thy
> name may be exalted through thy remembrance of God, the Creator of earth
> and heaven."** [54]

To William I, King of Prussia:

> **"Take heed lest pride debar thee from recognizing the Dayspring of Divine
> Revelation, lest earthly desires shut thee out, as by a veil, from the Lord of
> the Throne above and of the earth below."** [55]

To Francis-Joseph, the Austrian Emperor:

"Open thine eyes, that thou mayest behold this glorious Vision, and recognize Him Whom thou invokest in the daytime and in the night-season, and gaze on the Light that shineth above this luminous Horizon." [56]

To Sulṭán ʻAbduʼl-ʻAzíz of the Ottoman Empire:

"Lay not aside the fear of God, and be thou of them that act uprightly. Gather around thee those ministers from whom thou canst perceive the fragrance of faith and of justice, and take thou counsel with them, and choose whatever is best in thy sight, and be of them that act generously." [57]

To Náṣiriʼd-Dín Sháh of Persia:

"We pray that, out of His bounty—exalted be He—He may release, through this imprisonment, the necks of men from chains and fetters, and cause them to turn, with sincere faces, towards His Face, Who is the Mighty, the Bounteous. Ready is He to answer whosoever calleth upon Him, and nigh is He unto such as commune with Him." [58]

To the Rulers of America and the Presidents of its Republics:

"Bind ye the broken with the hands of justice, and crush the oppressor who flourisheth with the rod of the commandments of your Lord, the Ordainer, the All-Wise." [59]

To Pope Pius IX:

"The Word which the Son concealed is made manifest. It hath been sent down in the form of the human temple in this day. Blessed be the Lord Who is the Father! He, verily, is come unto the nations in His most great majesty." [60]

To the entire body of monks of the Christian Church:

"O concourse of monks! Seclude not yourselves in churches and cloisters. Come forth by My leave, and occupy yourselves with that which will profit your souls and the souls of men." [61]

SECTION 27

Four months after the sudden death of the Purest Branch, Baháʼuʼlláh and His companions had to be removed from the barracks to make way for some army troops. He and His family were placed in several houses for brief periods of time and finally moved into the house known today as the House of ʻAbbúd. They remained under watch and were surrounded by a population that, influenced by the orders of the Sulṭán, was unfriendly and hostile towards them.

With time, however, the people of 'Akká came to recognize the innocence of this small band of exiles from Persia, and the conditions of their confinement were eased. Much of the change was due to 'Abdu'l-Bahá, who was very much in contact with the inhabitants of the city and was able to demonstrate to them the true motives of the Bahá'ís and the spirit of His Father's Teachings. Eventually, Bahá'u'lláh could leave the city of 'Akká and visit nearby places. Having been confined so long in the walls of a desolate city, Bahá'u'lláh could now pass some time in the countryside and enjoy the beauty and greenery of nature He so loved.

The last years of Bahá'u'lláh's life were spent in the Mansion of Bahjí, just outside of 'Akká. Built while He was imprisoned within the city walls, it was abandoned by the owner when an epidemic broke out in the area. 'Abdu'l-Bahá was able to acquire it for His beloved Father, first renting it and later purchasing it outright.

By now the attitude of the people of not only 'Akká but also the nearby regions of Syria and Lebanon towards Bahá'u'lláh and His followers had completely changed. Though the orders of the Sultán were still in effect, and formally He was a prisoner under strict confinement, He, in reality, as revered and respected as a king. Even the officials of the region would come to seek His advice and counsel. Thus is the power of Bahá'u'lláh's Revelation to transform the hearts of men.

During the years in 'Akká and Bahjí, the Pen of Bahá'u'lláh revealed volumes and volumes of guidance that will enable humanity to build a glorious world civilization. The mightiest of the Works to flow from His Pen was the Kitáb-i-Aqdas, the Most Holy Book of His Dispensation, revealed in the House of 'Abbúd around 1873. Shoghi Effendi, referring to Bahá'u'lláh's Writings in the Holy Land, has said:

> **"The writings of Bahá'u'lláh during this period, as we survey the vast field which they embrace, seem to fall into three distinct categories. The first comprises those writings which constitute the sequel to the proclamation of His Mission in Adrianople. The second includes the laws and ordinances of His Dispensation, which, for the most part, have been recorded in the Kitáb-i-Aqdas, His Most Holy Book. To the third must be assigned those Tablets which partly enunciate and partly reaffirm the fundamental tenets and principles underlying that Dispensation."** [62]

The great expansion of the Faith of Bahá'u'lláh into the Western World did not begin during His own lifetime and would have to await the period of 'Abdu'l-Bahá's Ministry. His Teachings, however, had been introduced to countries of the West, and a few were aware of the Prisoner of 'Akká Who had remarkable influence on those with whom He came into contact. In the spring of 1890, towards the end of Bahá'u'lláh's life, Edward Granville Browne, a well-known scholar from Cambridge, England, came to meet Him. The following passages are from his record of that historic interview:

> ". . . my conductor paused for a moment while I removed my shoes. Then, with a quick movement of the hand, he withdrew, and, as I passed, replaced the curtain; and I found myself in a large apartment, along the upper end of which ran a low divan, while on the side opposite to the door were placed two or three chairs. Though I dimly suspected whither I was going and whom I was to behold (for no distinct intimation had been given to me), a second or two elapsed ere, with a throb of wonder and awe, I became definitely conscious that the room was not untenanted.

In the corner where the divan met the wall sat a wondrous and venerable figure, crowned with a felt head-dress of the kind called táj by dervishes (but of unusual height and make), round the base of which was wound a small white turban. The face of him on whom I gazed I can never forget, though I cannot describe it. Those piercing eyes seemed to read one's very soul; power and authority sat on that ample brow; while the deep lines on the forehead and face implied an age which the jet-black hair and beard flowing down in indistinguishable luxuriance almost to the waist seemed to belie. No need to ask in whose presence I stood, as I bowed myself before one who is the object of a devotion and love which kings might envy and emperors sigh for in vain!

"A mild dignified voice bade me be seated, and then continued:—**'Praise be to God that thou hast attained! . . . Thou hast come to see a prisoner and an exile . . . We desire but the good of the world and the happiness of the nations; yet they deem us a stirrer up of strife and sedition worthy of bondage and banishment . . . That all nations should become one in faith and all men as brothers; that the bonds of affection and unity between the sons of men should be strengthened; that diversity of religion should cease, and differences of race be annulled—what harm is there in this? . . . Yet so it shall be; these fruitless strifes, these ruinous wars shall pass away, and the 'Most Great Peace' shall come . . . Do not you in Europe need this also? Is not this that which Christ foretold? . . . Yet do we see your kings and rulers lavishing their treasures more freely on means for the destruction of the human race than on that which would conduce to the happiness of mankind . . . These strifes and this bloodshed and discord must cease, and all men be as one kindred and one family . . . Let not a man glory in this, that he loves his country; let him rather glory in this, that he loves his kind . . .'"** [63]

Exercises:

1. Under what circumstances were Bahá'u'lláh and His companions removed from the barracks? _____

2. What is the name of the house in 'Akká into which Bahá'u'lláh and His family finally moved? _____

3. How did the conditions of their life in 'Akká change? _____

   _____

4. What caused this change? _____

   _____

   _____

5. What is the name of the mansion where Bahá'u'lláh spent the last years of His life?

   _____

6. Under what circumstances did 'Abdu'l-Bahá acquire the Mansion of Bahjí? ____

   _____

7.   What is the most important Work revealed by Bahá'u'lláh during the years in 'Akká?

     _____

8.   Where was it revealed and when?_____

9.   What are the three categories into which, according to Shoghi Effendi, the Writings
     of Bahá'u'lláh during this period fall?

     a.   _____

          _____

     b.   _____

          _____

     c.   _____

          _____

10. What are some of the laws of Bahá'u'lláh's Dispensation? _____

     _____

     _____

     _____

     _____

11. What are some of the tenets and principles of His Dispensation?_____

     _____

     _____

     _____

     _____

12. Who was Edward Granville Browne? _____

     _____

13. Imagine that you are Edward Granville Browne and that you are at a gathering
     in England. Tell the story of your interview with Bahá'u'lláh with the necessary
     enthusiasm.

SECTION 28

The Kitáb-i-Aqdas is not a large book; it consists of only 190 paragraphs. In it,
however, are contained the basic laws and ordinances of the future world civilization.
Shoghi Effendi has referred to it as the Mother Book of Bahá'u'lláh's Dispensation and the

Charter of His New World Order. You will study passages from the Kitáb-i-Aqdas repeatedly throughout your life as you strive to align your thoughts and deeds with the commandments of God. For now, it is suggested that you memorize the opening five paragraphs.

"The first duty prescribed by God for His servants is the recognition of Him Who is the Dayspring of His Revelation and the Fountain of His laws, Who representeth the Godhead in both the Kingdom of His Cause and the world of creation. Whoso achieveth this duty hath attained unto all good; and whoso is deprived thereof hath gone astray, though he be the author of every righteous deed. It behooveth everyone who reacheth this most sublime station, this summit of transcendent glory, to observe every ordinance of Him Who is the Desire of the world. These twin duties are inseparable. Neither is acceptable without the other. Thus hath it been decreed by Him Who is the Source of Divine inspiration.

"They whom God hath endued with insight will readily recognize that the precepts laid down by God constitute the highest means for the maintenance of order in the world and the security of its peoples. He that turneth away from them is accounted among the abject and foolish. We, verily, have commanded you to refuse the dictates of your evil passions and corrupt desires, and not to transgress the bounds which the Pen of the Most High hath fixed, for these are the breath of life unto all created things. The seas of Divine wisdom and Divine utterance have risen under the breath of the breeze of the All-Merciful. Hasten to drink your fill, O men of understanding! They that have violated the Covenant of God by breaking His commandments, and have turned back on their heels, these have erred grievously in the sight of God, the All-Possessing, the Most High.

"O ye peoples of the world! Know assuredly that My commandments are the lamps of My loving providence among My servants, and the keys of My mercy for My creatures. Thus hath it been sent down from the heaven of the Will of your Lord, the Lord of Revelation. Were any man to taste the sweetness of the words which the lips of the All-Merciful have willed to utter, he would, though the treasures of the earth be in his possession, renounce them one and all, that he might vindicate the truth of even one of His commandments, shining above the Dayspring of His bountiful care and loving-kindness.

"Say: From My laws the sweet-smelling savor of My garment can be smelled, and by their aid the standards of Victory will be planted upon the highest peaks. The Tongue of My power hath, from the heaven of My omnipotent glory, addressed to My creation these words: 'Observe My commandments, for the love of My beauty.' Happy is the lover that hath inhaled the divine fragrance of his Best-Beloved from these words, laden with the perfume of a grace which no tongue can describe. By My life! He who hath drunk the choice wine of fairness from the hands of My bountiful favor will circle around My commandments that shine above the Dayspring of My creation.

"Think not that We have revealed unto you a mere code of laws. Nay, rather, We have unsealed the choice Wine with the fingers of might and power. To this beareth witness that which the Pen of Revelation hath revealed. Meditate upon this, O men of insight!" [64]

SECTION 29

Bahá'u'lláh's successive banishments, although apparently undertaken at the orders of worldly powers, were directed by the Hand of Almighty God Himself. The spiritual forces released as the Manifestation of God moved from place to place, finally arriving in the Holy Land where the spiritual and administrative center of His Faith was to be established, are incalculable. Below is a map showing the route of His exiles. You should commit to memory its details and have firmly engraved in your mind the image of the path that took Him from Iran to the Holy Land.

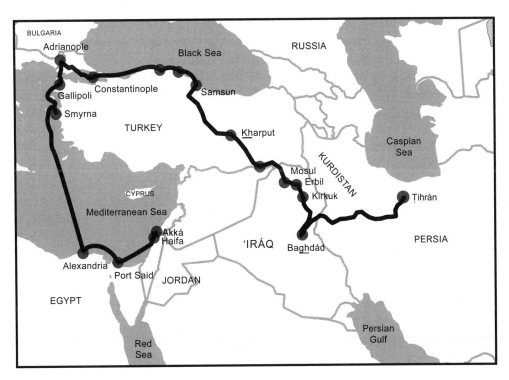

SECTION 30

During the years that a Manifestation of God walks among men, His extraordinary powers are diffused throughout the world, causing a profound change in the reality of all created things. In this Glorious Day, Bahá'u'lláh revealed the Word of God to humanity for almost forty years, endowing the world of being with limitless potentialities, the unfoldment of which will give rise to a civilization of unimaginable beauty. These forty years of continuous Divine Revelation came to an end on 29 May 1892.

Nine months before His ascension, Bahá'u'lláh had expressed His desire to depart from this world. From that time on, it became increasingly clear from the tone of the remarks He made, that the close of His life on this earthly plane was approaching. On the night of 8 May 1892, He contracted a slight fever. The fever grew the following day, but then seemed to go away. He continued to allow certain of the friends and pilgrims to meet with Him, but it soon became evident that He was not well. His fever returned, this time stronger than before, and His condition slowly grew worse. At the hour of dawn on 29 May 1892, in the 75th year of His life, His spirit ascended from this world.

Six days before He passed away, He called to His presence all the believers assembled in the Mansion of Bahjí, for what was to be their last meeting with Him. As He lay in bed supported by one of His sons, He addressed them. "I am well pleased with you all," He said. "Ye have rendered many services, and been very assiduous in your labors. Ye have come here every morning and every evening. May God assist you to remain united. May He aid you to exalt the Cause of the Lord of being." [65] Tears streamed from the eyes of those gathered around Him.

News of His passing was immediately communicated to the Sulṭán by telegram. The message began with the words "the Sun of Bahá has set" and went on to inform the Sulṭán of the plans to bury the sacred remains near the Mansion. A small room in a house just west of the Mansion was selected, and shortly after sunset on the very day of His ascension, His Body was laid to rest. The Qiblih of the people of Bahá was now fixed at this Holy Spot. Nabíl describes the agony of those days in these words: "Methinks, the spiritual commotion set up in the world of dust had caused all the worlds of God to tremble. . . . My inner and outer tongue are powerless to portray the condition we were in. . . . In the midst of the prevailing confusion a multitude of the inhabitants of ʻAkká and of the neighboring villages, that had thronged the fields surrounding the Mansion, could be seen weeping, beating upon their heads, and crying aloud their grief." [66]

For a full week, large numbers of mourners, rich and poor alike, came to express their grief to Bahá'u'lláh's family. Prominent people from all segments of society, including Muslims, Christians and Jews, poets, clergy and government officials, joined in sorrowing over His loss and in praising His virtues and greatness. Many of them even paid written tributes to Him. Similar tributes were received from cities throughout the region, all of which were submitted to ʻAbdu'l-Bahá, who now represented the Cause of Bahá'u'lláh. However, these expressions of sorrow were, in the words of the Guardian, "but a drop when compared with the ocean of grief and the innumerable evidences of unbounded devotion which, at the hour of the setting of the Sun of Truth, poured forth from the hearts of the countless thousands who had espoused His Cause, and were determined to carry aloft its banner in Persia, India, Russia, ʻIráq, Turkey, Palestine, Egypt and Syria." [67]

Exercise:

1.   Present to your group an account of the ascension of Bahá'u'lláh in your own words.

SECTION 31

After Bahá'u'lláh's passing, Nabíl was chosen by ʻAbdu'l-Bahá to select those passages that make up the text of the Tablet of Visitation. This Tablet is recited in the Shrines of Bahá'u'lláh and the Báb. It is also frequently used in commemorating Their anniversaries. The Ascension of Bahá'u'lláh is commemorated in the early hours of 29 May. You will, of course, be an active supporter of such gatherings in your community and should therefore be well familiar with the text of this Tablet of utmost beauty.

"The praise which hath dawned from Thy most august Self, and the glory which hath shone forth from Thy most effulgent Beauty, rest upon Thee, O

Thou Who art the Manifestation of Grandeur, and the King of Eternity, and the Lord of all who are in heaven and on earth! I testify that through Thee the sovereignty of God and His dominion, and the majesty of God and His grandeur, were revealed, and the Daystars of ancient splendor have shed their radiance in the heaven of Thine irrevocable decree, and the Beauty of the Unseen hath shone forth above the horizon of creation. I testify, moreover, that with but a movement of Thy Pen Thine injunction 'Be Thou' hath been enforced, and God's hidden Secret hath been divulged, and all created things have been called into being, and all the Revelations have been sent down.

"I bear witness, moreover, that through Thy beauty the beauty of the Adored One hath been unveiled, and through Thy face the face of the Desired One hath shone forth, and that through a word from Thee Thou hast decided between all created things, causing them who are devoted to Thee to ascend unto the summit of glory, and the infidels to fall into the lowest abyss.

"I bear witness that he who hath known Thee hath known God, and he who hath attained unto Thy presence hath attained unto the presence of God. Great, therefore, is the blessedness of him who hath believed in Thee, and in Thy signs, and hath humbled himself before Thy sovereignty, and hath been honored with meeting Thee, and hath attained the good pleasure of Thy will, and circled around Thee, and stood before Thy throne. Woe betide him that hath transgressed against Thee, and hath denied Thee, and repudiated Thy signs, and gainsaid Thy sovereignty, and risen up against Thee, and waxed proud before Thy face, and hath disputed Thy testimonies, and fled from Thy rule and Thy dominion, and been numbered with the infidels whose names have been inscribed by the fingers of Thy behest upon Thy holy Tablets.

"Waft, then, unto me, O my God and my Beloved, from the right hand of Thy mercy and Thy loving-kindness, the holy breaths of Thy favors, that they may draw me away from myself and from the world unto the courts of Thy nearness and Thy presence. Potent art Thou to do what pleaseth Thee. Thou, truly, hast been supreme over all things.

"The remembrance of God and His praise, and the glory of God and His splendor, rest upon Thee, O Thou Who art His Beauty! I bear witness that the eye of creation hath never gazed upon one wronged like Thee. Thou wast immersed all the days of Thy life beneath an ocean of tribulations. At one time Thou wast in chains and fetters; at another Thou wast threatened by the sword of Thine enemies. Yet, despite all this, Thou didst enjoin upon all men to observe what had been prescribed unto Thee by Him Who is the All-Knowing, the All-Wise.

"May my spirit be a sacrifice to the wrongs Thou didst suffer, and my soul be a ransom for the adversities Thou didst sustain. I beseech God, by Thee and by them whose faces have been illumined with the splendors of the light of Thy countenance, and who, for love of Thee, have observed all whereunto they were bidden, to remove the veils that have come in between Thee and Thy creatures, and to supply me with the good of this world and the world to come. Thou art, in truth, the Almighty, the Most Exalted, the All-Glorious, the Ever-Forgiving, the Most Compassionate.

"Bless Thou, O Lord my God, the Divine Lote-Tree and its leaves, and its boughs, and its branches, and its stems, and its offshoots, as long as Thy most excellent titles will endure and Thy most august attributes will last. Protect it, then, from the mischief of the aggressor and the hosts of tyranny. Thou art, in truth, the Almighty, the Most Powerful. Bless Thou, also, O Lord my God, Thy servants and Thy handmaidens who have attained unto Thee. Thou, truly, art the All-Bountiful, Whose grace is infinite. No God is there save Thee, the Ever-Forgiving, the Most Generous." [68]

SECTION 32

From your own experience, you know that you will have numerous opportunities in the years to come to tell the story of Bahá'u'lláh's life. The account of His life which you have now studied is more detailed than the one that was presented in Book 2. You will be able to use your new knowledge, in varying degrees, as you engage in teaching activities. There will be many occasions when a simple presentation is called for, especially in the deepening of newly enrolled believers. The following pages will assist you in this task.

Bahá'u'lláh

The Glory of God

Bahá'u'lláh was born on 12 November 1817 in Ṭihrán, the capital of Iran. From His childhood, He showed signs of greatness. He received some instruction at home, but did not need to attend school, for He was endowed by God with innate knowledge.

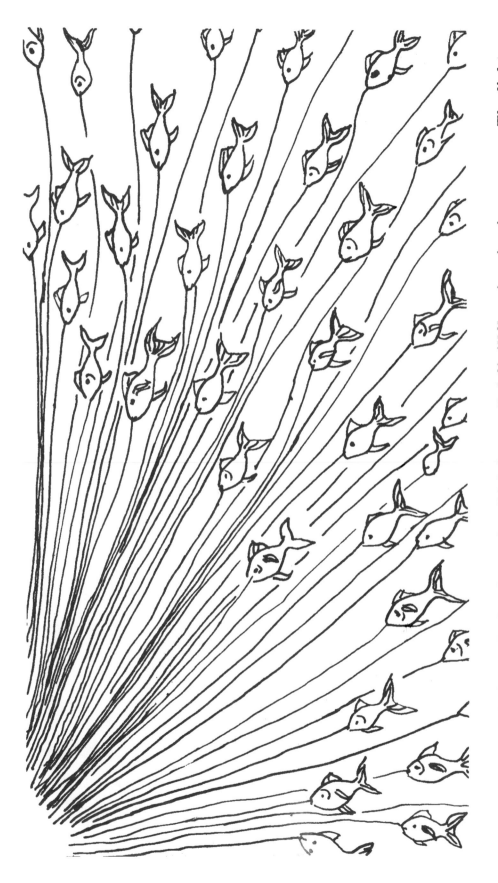

One night, His father had a dream in which he saw Bahá'u'lláh swimming in an ocean. The light radiating from His body illuminated the waters. His long black hair floated in all directions, and a multitude of fish followed Him, each holding on to the end of one hair. He moved freely and unhindered. This dream was one of the many indications of the great destiny that awaited Bahá'u'lláh.

2

Later when He was a young man, He was offered a high position in the court of the King, but He refused it. He wished to dedicate His time to helping the oppressed, the sick and the poor, and to champion the cause of justice.

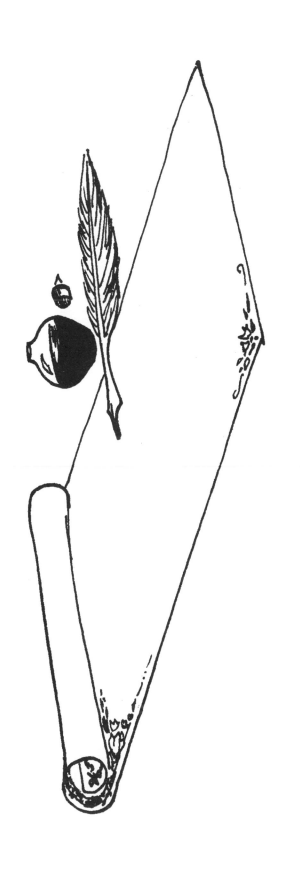

When He was 27 years old, Bahá'u'lláh received a scroll of Writings from the Báb, the new Messenger of God, Who was preparing the people for the coming of the Promise of All Ages. Bahá'u'lláh accepted the Báb's Message and became one of His most enthusiastic supporters.

The authorities, unwilling to accept the Truth proclaimed by the Báb, set out to persecute those who believed in Him, and thus began the sufferings of Bahá'u'lláh. In the year 1852, He was arrested and put in chains in one of the most dreadful prisons of Ṭihrán.

5

In this prison, God revealed to Bahá'u'lláh that He was the One promised by the Báb and all the Prophets of the past. From this dark dungeon rose the Sun of Truth, illuminating the world and giving birth to a new Day in the life of humanity.

After four months of imprisonment, the government banished Bahá'u'lláh from His native land. During the bitter cold of winter, Bahá'u'lláh and His family made the long journey from Ṭihrán to Baghdád.

7

In Baghdád, the fame of Bahá'u'lláh's wisdom spread in all directions. People of every background crowded to His home, seeking His help and advice. The government, which was afraid of Bahá'u'lláh's influence, decided to banish Him even farther from His homeland.

8

21 April 1863

Before leaving Baghdád, Bahá'u'lláh spent twelve days in a garden outside the city, where streams of visitors came to bid Him farewell. In this garden, Bahá'u'lláh proclaimed that He was the Manifestation of God for this Day. For centuries to come, the period of 21 April to 2 May will be celebrated as the Festival of Riḍván, the anniversary of the Declaration of Bahá'u'lláh of His world-embracing Mission.

Napoleon III, the
Emperor of the French

William I
King of Prussia

Franz-Joseph
the Austrian Emperor

Queen Victoria
of England

Nicolaevitch Alexander II
the Czar of Russia

Pope Pius IX

Sultán 'Abdu'l-Aziz
of the Ottoman Empire

Náṣiri'd-Dín Sháh
of Persia

Bahá'u'lláh's next place of exile was Constantinople and later, Adrianople, both cities in today's Turkey. From Adrianople, Bahá'u'lláh, a prisoner and an exile, sent letters to the kings and rulers of the world bidding them to uphold justice and to use their power to put an end to misery and war.

10

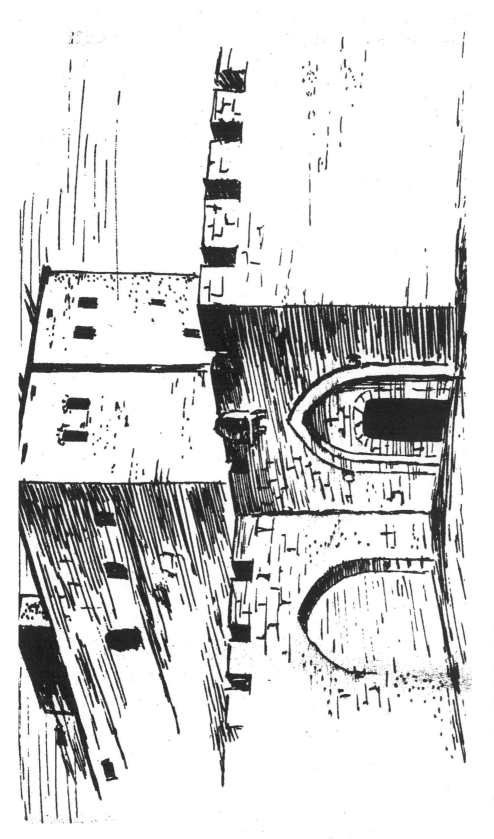

Once again, Bahá'u'lláh's fame spread among the inhabitants of the region, and the government decided to banish Him even farther away to the prison-city of 'Akká. This was the prison to which the worst criminals and agitators of the land were sent, never to be heard of again.

11

The conditions of imprisonment were extremely severe. Some of the followers of Bahá'u'lláh travelled great distances to 'Akká, but were not allowed to enter His presence. They could only catch a glimpse of Him from afar as He waved to them from the window of His prison-cell.

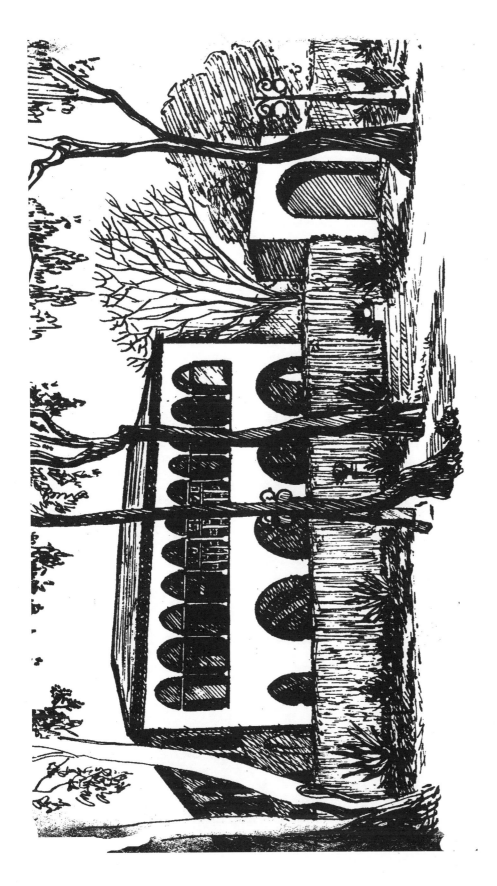

Gradually conditions improved as the power of Bahá'u'lláh's words and deeds conquered the hearts of high and low alike. During the last years of His life, He lived in the Mansion of Bahjí outside the city walls. In 'Akká, Bahá'u'lláh revealed volumes of guidance for humanity, including the Kitáb-i-Aqdas, His Most Holy Book.

13

In May 1892 Bahá'u'lláh passed away. His resting place in Bahjí, now surrounded by beautiful gardens, is the most Holy Spot on earth. 'Akká and the nearby city of Haifa are the spiritual and administrative center of the Bahá'í community which is striving to bring about the World Order of Bahá'u'lláh and the prosperity of humankind.

14

REFERENCES

1. *The Promulgation of Universal Peace: Talks Delivered by 'Abdu'l-Bahá during His Visit to the United States and Canada in 1912* (Wilmette: Bahá'í Publishing Trust, 1995), p. 25.

2. Bahá'u'lláh, *The Summons of the Lord of Hosts: Tablets of Bahá'u'lláh* (Haifa: Bahá'í World Centre, 2002), p. 167.

3. Ibid., pp. 167-68.

4. *The Dawn-Breakers: Nabíl's Narrative of the Early Days of the Bahá'í Revelation* (Wilmette: Bahá'í Publishing Trust, 1974), p. 119.

5. *The Dawn-Breakers*, pp. 119-20.

6. Bahá'u'lláh, *Epistle to the Son of the Wolf* (Wilmette: Bahá'í Publishing Trust, 1995), p. 11.

7. *'Abdu'l-Bahá on Divine Philosphy* (Boston: Tudor Press, 1918), p. 49.

8. *The Dawn-Breakers*, p. 96.

9. Ibid., p. 104.

10. Ibid., pp. 104-05.

11. Ibid., pp. 105-06.

12. Ibid., p. 106.

13. Ibid., p. 107.

14. Ibid., p. 107.

15. Ibid., pp. 107-08.

16. *Selections from the Writings of the Báb* (Haifa: Bahá'í World Centre, 1982), pp. 82-83.

17. Ibid., p. 98.

18. Ibid., p. 149.

19. *The Dawn-Breakers*, p. 113.

20. Ibid., p. 116.

21. *Gleanings from the Writings of Bahá'u'lláh* (Wilmette: Bahá'í Publishing Trust, 1994), CXXIX, pp. 279-80.

22.   *The Promulgation of Universal Peace*, pp. 141-42.

23.   From a letter dated 29 August 1852 written by Captain Von Goumoens, cited in Shoghi Effendi, *God Passes By* (Wilmette: Bahá'í Publishing Trust, 1995), pp. 65-66.

24.   *The Dawn-Breakers*, pp. 607-08.

25.   *Tablets of Bahá'u'lláh Revealed after the Kitáb-i-Aqdas* (Wilmette: Bahá'í Publishing Trust, 1994), p. 40.

26.   Ibid., p. 96.

27.   *The Dawn-Breakers*, p. 632.

28.   *Epistle to the Son of the Wolf*, pp. 20-21.

29.   *The Dawn-Breakers*, pp. 631-33.

30.   *Epistle to the Son of the Wolf*, p. 21.

31.   Ibid., p. 22.

32.   *God Passes By*, pp. 101-02.

33.   *Gleanings from the Writings of Bahá'u'lláh*, XXIX, p. 72.

34.   From a letter dated 24 June 1936 written on behalf of Shoghi Effendi to an individual believer, cited in the compilation, *Crisis and Victory* (London: Bahá'í Publishing Trust, 1988), p. 15.

35.   Balyuzi, H.M., *Bahá'u'lláh: The King of Glory* (Oxford: George Ronald, 1991), p. 104.

36.   Bahá'u'lláh, cited in *God Passes By*, p. 109.

37.   Bahá'u'lláh, *The Kitáb-i-Íqán* (Wilmette: Bahá'í Publishing Trust, 1993), p. 251.

38.   *God Passes By*, p. 115.

39.   Ibid., p. 137.

40.   *Epistle to the Son of the Wolf*, p. 22.

41.   *God Passes By*, p. 144.

42.   *The Kitáb-i-Íqán*, p. 3.

43.   Bahá'u'lláh, *The Hidden Words* (Wilmette: Bahá'í Publishing Trust, 1994), p. 3.

44.   *God Passes By*, p. 147.

45. Bahá'u'lláh, *The Kitáb-i-Aqdas: The Most Holy Book* (Wilmette: Bahá'í Publishing Trust, 1993), p. 48.

46. *God Passes By*, p. 153.

47. *Gleanings from the Writings of Bahá'u'lláh*, XIV, pp. 27-32.

48. *God Passes By*, p. 160.

49. Bahá'u'lláh, cited in *God Passes By*, p. 185.

50. *Bahá'u'lláh: The King of Glory*, pp. 311-13.

51. Bahá'u'lláh, cited in *God Passes By*, p. 184.

52. *The Proclamation of Bahá'u'lláh to the Kings and Leaders of the World* (Haifa: Bahá'í World Centre, 1967), p. 17.

53. Ibid., p. 28.

54. Ibid., p. 33.

55. Ibid., p. 39.

56. Ibid., p. 43.

57. Ibid., p. 47.

58. Ibid., p. 60.

59. Ibid., p. 63.

60. Ibid., p. 84.

61. Ibid., p. 95.

62. *God Passes By*, pp. 205-06.

63. *Bahá'u'lláh: The King of Glory*, pp. 371-73.

64. *The Kitáb-i-Aqdas: The Most Holy Book*, pp. 21-23.

65. *God Passes By*, p. 222.

66. Ibid., p. 222.

67. Ibid., p. 223.

68. Bahá'u'lláh, *Bahá'í Prayers: A Selection of Prayers Revealed by Bahá'u'lláh, the Báb, and 'Abdu'l-Bahá* (Wilmette: Bahá'í Publishing Trust, 1993), pp. 230-33.